Swept Out of a Dead Frontier:
Apocalypse, Disappearance
and the Uncertain Future
of the Contemporary Western

Swept Out of a Dead Frontier: Apocalypse, Disappearance and the Uncertain Future of the Contemporary Western

Jeremy T. Wattles

Swept Out of a Dead Frontier:
Apocalypse, Disappearance and the
Uncertain Future of the
Contemporary Western

Copyright © 2013
by Jeremy T. Wattles

cover design by Lucy Swerdfeger

All rights reserved. No part of this book may be used or reproduced in any manner whatsoever without written permission from the publisher, except in the case of brief quotations embodied in articles and reviews.

Published by

~Star Cloud Press®~
6137 East Mescal Street
Scottsdale, Arizona 85254-5418

StarCloudPress.com

Paperback — 978-1-932842-68-5 — $ 14.95

Printed in the United States of America

For my parents:
who got me there and back,
and for Erik:
who got me through.

Table of Contents

Acknowledgments	-i-
Apocalypse and The Contemporary West	1
I: From the New World to New Western History and Literature	12
II: Annie Proulx	22
III: Cormac McCarthy	32
IV: Sherman Alexie	39
Beyond Apocalypse — Western Places and Myths in the 21st Century	46
Notes	57
Works Cited and Consulted	64
About the Author	69

Acknowledgments

Most of all, I express thanks and appreciation to thank Dr. Ken Millard, who first introduced me to the topic of Western Fictions when I was a visiting international student studying at the University of Edinburgh and had the unplanned good fortune of being placed in his seminar. At a difficult time in my life, his class was one of the few things I found interesting and invigorating. It was a place where I was delighted to read an eclectic selection of novels and to discuss their themes and greater cultural resonances. I also learned an invaluable amount about myself and my relationship to American culture. It was one of the pleasant paradoxes of traveling and studying abroad, of being so tangibly removed from a familiar context and national ideology, yet thereby enabled to grasp anew its basic assumptions and their subsequent implications. Dr. Millard has since proven to be a trusted mentor and confidant.

I must also acknowledge Dr. Adam Budd's Research Methods class as helpful, interesting and enlightening. Thanks also to my parents, who provided helpful insights. In addition, I extend deepest thanks to my classmate and friend Erik Jaccard for his challenging questions and critique of the first draft of this dissertation. Finally, thank you to Dr. Steven Swerdfeger, another confidant and advisor—for his patience with me in bringing this critical study to publication and for his willingness and generosity to see the project through.

"I discovered that I was not opposed to mankind but man-centeredness, anthropocentricity, the opinion that the world exists solely for the sake of man; not to science, which means simply knowledge, but science misapplied, to the worship of technique and technology, and to that perversion of science properly called scientism; and not to civilization but culture."
— Edward Abbey, *Desert Solitaire*

"I operate under the idea that we are all full of shit…[we are all] fragile and finite."
—Sherman Alexie, in a lecture given at Colgate University, 2004

"This is the way the world ends
Not with a bang but a whimper."
— T. S. Eliot, "The Hollow Men"

Apocalypse and The Contemporary West

In her 1989 book *Writing the Apocalypse: Historical Vision in Contemporary U.S. and Latin American Fiction* Lois Parkinson Zamora argued that apocalypse "is used again and again to refer to the events of recent history...the end of this millennium has displaced 1984 as a focus of speculation, and apocalypse is in vogue."[1]

Apocalypse is certainly still in vogue in the early years of the new millennium, especially in contemporary fiction of the American West. Authors such as Cormac McCarthy, Sherman Alexie and Annie Proulx have all published books with strong eschatological tropes in the last few years. Whether they have been focused on specific historical moments like September 11, 2001, or preoccupied with wider cultural, ethical, ecological and mythological disintegrations, an overarching sense of dissipation and forthcoming disaster remains present in their work. In other words, these authors have called into question mythic American notions of progress, freedom, history and vitality in the Western setting in very specific and dire terms, terms which subsequently pose crucial questions about what kind of future remains for Americans in their often idealized and misunderstood West.

This critical study will focus on three works, Annie Proulx's *Bad Dirt: Wyoming Stories 2* (2004), Cormac McCarthy's *No Country for Old Men* (2005), and Sherman Alexie's *The Lone Ranger and Tonto Fistfight in Heaven* (1993). Specifically, I will examine how these three works evoke a sense of apocalypse and will discuss some of the implications of these apocalyptic moments in relation to the larger concerns of contemporary Western fiction and some of its inter-disciplinary concerns. I will also compare these works to the larger historical context of apocalyptic literature and the origins of American national identity, using Zamora and Frank Kermode's *The Sense of an Ending* (1967) as my critical starting points.

First it will be useful define, for the purposes of this argument, both "The West" and "Apocalypse." The West as a term is a confused, conflated, multivalent mess, shot through with centuries of interconnected significations. Larry McMurtry does an admirable job, however, of defining three key conceptions of the West his essay collection *Sacagawea's Nickname* (2001):

> ...when we talk about the West we may be talking about three entities at once: the historical West, the geographical West, and the psychological West, or what one might call the West-in-the-mind's-eye. These three Wests are interwoven in patterns that are confusing and indistinct...No matter how hard historians try to focus on the historic West or the geographic West, the West-in-the-mind's-eye subtly but almost invariably intrudes.[2]

Within each of these there are subdivisions; the historical West has to address issues of conquest, genocide, and the politics of expansion; the geographical size of the West was continually changing for the majority of North American history; the West-in-the-mind's-eye invariably conjures up notions of the cowboy's seemingly intrinsic freedom, of Western settlers starting anew, etc. In any case, as McMurtry correctly argues, the most potent of all the Wests is the psychological, or what I would also refer to as the mythological West, the West that has spread around the globe and remains vital even if all the American wilderness is someday mapped, populated, privatized and despoiled.

It is this psychological West that best applies to Proulx, McCarthy, and Alexie. Consider Sherman Alexie—he may incorporate elements of geography and history to flesh out settings and characters, but it is the realm of dreams and ideas, of imagination and subsequent action that he explores in order to, as Kermode says "help us make sense of our lives."[3] A passage from "Imagining the Reservation," reveals such an interwoven pattern:

> What do you believe in? Does every Indian depend on Hollywood for a twentieth-century vision? Listen: when I was young, living on the reservation, eating potatoes every day of my life, I imagined the potatoes grew larger, filled my stomach, reversed the emptiness.[4]

Alexie objects to the psychological West that Hollywood's culture industry spews out and sets his own imagination against it. His call to *listen* is an appeal for authority and authenticity, and when he says emptiness, the word resonates on all three of McMurtry's levels, bodily hunger aside.

As for apocalypse, it is important to understand that we are talking about a term stretching back beyond any Christian sense of the end of the world, or the capital "A" Apocalypse. We are talking about apocalypse with a small "a," about *an* end to a particular epoch, a particular lifetime, or a particular idea, not *The* End. As Zamora argues, "Apocalypse is *not* merely a synonym for disaster or cataclysm or chaos. It is, in fact, a synonym for 'revelation.'" Her etymological discussion is illuminating:

> The word itself originally derives from the Greek word *apocalypsis*, to uncover, reveal, disclose (the root is *kalypto*, to cover or conceal...familiar to us in the name of the nymph Calypso, who hides Odysseus for seven years). Apocalypse is eschatological in nature (the root in this case is *eschatos*, furthest or uttermost); it is concerned with final things, with the end of the present age and with the age to follow.[5]

Thus, when applied to literature, and subsequently to critical theory, the discourse concerning apocalypse attempts to reveal the true nature of our cosmological place in time through storytelling. This can be a frightening prospect; quite often we encounter the notion that our lives have no universal meaning other than that which we invent for them.

Frank Kermode tested the artistic validity of apocalyptic fiction in his seminal critical study *The Sense of an Ending*. He observed that "men, like poets, rush 'into the middest,' *in medias res*, when they are born; they also die *in mediis rebus*, and to make sense of their span, they need fictive concords with origins and ends, such as give meaning to lives and to poems."[6] This need to instill significance in one's own life is a condition irrespective of time, a constant from the earliest surviving stories down to the present day.

In the absence of any verifiable teleology to our existence or our universe, all life becomes, in one sense, a fiction of arbitrary, personal timescales. It is a fiction of synthetic understanding and fantastic escape—it can hold both our troublesome uncertainties and our delusions of importance in a single moment. Scientist, atheist, or believer, we project Beginning and End onto time's immense and incomprehensible face, often feeling anxiety that we are living in the last days. These "fundamentally arbitrary chronological divisions…are made to bear the weight of our anxieties and hopes…they help us to find ends and beginnings. They explain our senescence, our renovations."[7] From scripture to Spenser to Sartre, Kermode charts this apocalyptic trope; he argues that this has manifested itself in every generation, and especially in 1000, 1400, 1600, and 1900, which was, until recent millennial concerns, the archetypal *fin de siecle*.[8] Hence the sustained and intense examination of history throughout the movements and moments of literature. As such, while McCarthyian musings about the end of the world may seem dire, eschatological anxiety is anything but a recent literary theme.

But what about our own time? Despite a scientifically enriched understanding of time and its workings in relation to the universe, and despite deep fears concerning humanity's sustainable future in the wake of the sheer environmental destruction, the brutality, and the bloodshed of the twentieth century, Kermode questions the singularity of our situation. While it may be "commonplace to talk about our historical situation as uniquely terrible and in a way privileged, a cardinal point in time…can it really be so?" In the Middle Ages, people were terrified that "armies in the sky…or a palpable Antichrist" would visit destruction and judgment upon them, and it is essentially sophistry to claim that "nuclear bombs are more real and make one experience more authentic crisis-feelings."[9] We cannot gainsay the dead. Or, to quote Auden: "The Tyranny of the Dead. One cannot react against them."[10]

It is humbling to consider that there is "nothing at all distinguishing about eschatological anxiety;" it pervades human history.[11] What has changed is its artistic valence. While the OED defines eschatology as "the department of theological science concerned with 'the four last things: death, judgment, heaven and hell,'" contemporary literature employs a looser, metaphorical definition.[12] Because the precise temporal moment of the end has been constantly expected but perpetually deferred, because science has increasingly challenged theology and that moment has become less certain, the resonance of the Apocalypse has shifted from the actual to the imagined. Kermode makes the vital distinction clear: "although the end has perhaps for us lost its naïve imminence, its shadow still lies on the crises of our fictions; we may speak of it as immanent."[13] Critically regarded, self-reflexive literature acknowledges this difference, and uses apocalyptic themes, symbols, and images not to describe a literal end of the world, but to call for an immanent end. This revelatory process, rather than a disconnected destructive moment, presents a more sophisticated eschatology. For Annie Proulx, the Four Horsemen no longer threaten to sweep through old Wyoming ghost towns to lay waste the country, but they remain within the mind of the author and her characters like a recurring nightmare, signaling to us different kinds of imminence. Apocalypse can signify smaller endings such as the end of a life, the end of a ranch, the extinction of a species or the flooding of a canyon in the wilderness.

Thus Kermode provides aesthetic criteria by which we may judge contemporary fictions. Lois Parkinson Zamora extends this argument in *Writing the Apocalypse* (1989), writing that authors use apocalypse to "confront cultural and political corruption," and to challenge history.[14]

In keeping with this aesthetic rubric, fiction can be eschatological when it exposes history's illusions and its elisions; it can re-write a faulty history or reveal and confront its persistent myths. In a paradoxical move, fiction takes on history's role, exposing history's own fictional tendencies. Not all historians strive for honesty, and even those who do may be prone to false evidence and personal prejudice. If the victors are the writers of history, a novel like McCarthy's *Blood Meridian* (1985) reveals those writers as depraved butchers, shattering all illusions of a benign Manifest Destiny. In other words, authors such as Proulx, McCarthy, and Alexie, who are opposed to official versions of history, precipitate a necessary dialogical space though their very work. Their fiction allows for history's losers to enter into a critical debate, fueling what New Western Historian P.N. Limerick, in *The Legacy of Conquest* (1987), calls a part of the inherent and continued "competition for legitimacy" in the American West. This competition is "accompanied by a contest for cultural dominance," and, Limerick argues, is "reconceived as a running story, a fragmented and discontinuous past [which] becomes whole again."[15]

With these working definitions of "The West" and "apocalypse" in mind, I will offer brief summaries of significant plot points and themes for each of my three chosen authors. Then I will return to the geographic West, in a brief attempt to show a point of convergence between the two terms. This will begin to ground these somewhat abstract concepts in the texts themselves, and will facilitate further critical discussion.

Annie Proulx's recent short story collection *Bad Dirt: Wyoming Stories 2* (2004) offers a bleak account of the contemporary American West. Consider this passage from "What Kind of Furniture Would Jesus Pick?"—

> By the end of the century Gilbert was fifty-five and caught in the downward ranching spiral of too much work, not enough money, drought. It kept getting drier and drier, grasshoppers appearing as early as April and

promising a plague in August. The grass cracked like eggshells under his feet. There was no color in the landscape, the alkali dust muting sage, grass, stones, the earth itself. When a vehicle passed along the road a fine cloud spread out and slowly settled. The air was baked of scent except for the chalky dust with its faint odor of old cardboard. He was conscious of how many things could go wrong, of how poorly he'd reckoned the ranch's problems.[16]

More than bleak, there is a menacing, apocalyptic slant to the diction and imagery, a marshalling of eschatological tropes against mythic Western ideals. This lone man, Gilbert Wolfscale, finds it increasingly difficult to maintain even the illusory appearance of self-reliance. He is beset by plagues and a desiccated, uninhabitable land; in place of economic success in a fertile New World, and emotional fulfillment in the psychological/philosophical open range of the West, there are only aborted promises, cracked like eggshells. Gilbert may be alone on his ranch and with his thoughts, but he shares his quiet desperation with most of Proulx's characters. They live unfulfilled, squalid, and pathetically comic lives, grounded in what the New York *Times* review of the collection calls "stubborn futility". Furthermore, Proulx's interest in Wyoming as a source for her art may be ending. Terrence Rafferty suggests that Proulx's "impatience" with the lives of the characters she describes has caused some of her fiction to degenerate into sloppy, misanthropic "local color."[17] We must ask, then, if Proulx's harsh, tragic-comic portrayal of Wyoming in *Bad Dirt* is justified, and examine what other causes there are for her negative outlook on the West.

Cormac McCarthy's novel, *No Country For Old Men* (2005), takes its title from the opening line of W.B. Yeats', "Sailing to Byzantium" (1928). In that first line, Yeats "repudiat[es] a Gaelic tradition of poetic praise of Ireland in terms of her beauty and fecundity."[18] The poet journeys from Ireland to Byzantium, on an "alchemical quest" for spiritual "transfiguration" from the aging body's "decrepitude."[19] If McCarthy's view of the American West is consonant with Yeats's negative, transient view of Ireland, does McCarthy also offer his characters a voyage away? If so, is it one of renewal? McCarthy's eschatological choice also implies an urgency lacking from his previous titles. While he has entitled some of his other novels with biblical phrases, like *Child of God* (1974) and *Outer Dark* (1968), those novels do not have Western settings, nor has McCarthy specifically recalled an apocalyptic, violent and post-Christian poet such as Yeats. This novel tells of a chase for drug money along the Texas-Mexico border in the wake of the Vietnam War, in which there is the persistent sense that the law cannot cope with late twentieth century criminals, nor are there any more mythic, regenerating quests to set out upon. In McCarthy's harsh universe, there may be no ships sailing to Byzantium, no artifice of eternity in which the soul may abide. Instead, characters suffer a weakening of their authority and potency in an indifferent and harsh land; they will either die out with a whimper or be hounded into a corner, slaughtered by a new breed of amoral and superior killers.

Myth is also the target of apocalyptic revaluation in Sherman Alexie's *The Lone Ranger and Tonto Fistfight in Heaven* (1993). His relentless attack on Western myths, beginning with his subversive title, seeks to bring their spurious, absurd reign to an end by showing how they have jettisoned history and subjugated Native Americans. Alexie's interconnected short stories also consider the disturbing possibility of the end of the tribe via the alcoholic, economic dead end of reservation life, or potential assimilation into the white world. Resistance, through acts of writing and storytelling, may help preserve and articulate Indian identity, but this resistance is hard-won. Andrew Dix suggests that Alexie's acts of storytelling "emerge within situations of loss." Rather than face that loss, Alexie's characters often treat storytelling as a "psychotic compulsion," something "anachronistic, even obsolete."[20] It is sometimes less painful for them to remain, paralyzed and passive, on the reservation than confront the freight of history and envision a hopeful, dynamic future for the Spokane community. However, this forgetful, fixed attitude toward storytelling and survival is like an opiate, unrewarding and escapist. To tell a good story, one that "puts wood in the fireplace," Alexie's characters must imagine and enact a more organic type of storytelling, for it is the best way to ensure the survival of Indian identity and culture.[21] Consequently, Sherman Alexie's tribal traditions and memories will not be consigned to oblivion, or mythologized into a mysterious apotheosis of disappearance like the Anasazi.

While it is obvious that all three authors demonstrate considerable focus on the psycho-historical aspects of the West's myths and metaphors, it is important to highlight their parallel focus on the environmental/geographic facet of the West. Certainly each author has particular interests and details they wish to portray pertaining to their regional setting and its characters. Yet they also acknowledge in their respective works an interconnected nation and world, and all three authors share fundamentally similar apocalyptic warnings regarding economics and environment that resonate outside the sphere of literature itself. Many scientists corroborate this seemingly exponential process of culture devouring nature. For example, Jared Diamond devotes his first chapter of *Collapse* (2005) to a study of Montana, which he calls "a microcosm of the environmental problems plaguing the rest of the United States". His eschatological title and subsequent descriptions of the West stand in stark contrast to our popular idea of America as full of limitless resources. Even in the lush Bitteroot Valley there is the potential for cataclysmic collapse or ecocide:

> ...seemingly pristine Montana actually suffers from serious environmental problems involving toxic wastes, forests, soils, water, climate change, biodiversity losses, and introduced pests. All these problems translate into economic problems. They provide much of the explanation for why Montana's economy has been declining in recent decades to the point where what was formerly one of our richest states is now one of the poorest.[22]

Thus, ecological collapse may be an imminent end. Proulx's "downward ranching spiral," McCarthy's unforgiving West Texas desert, and Alexie's dead-end life on the rez are not specious—they are the literary expressions of tangible difficulties facing contemporary Westerners. Furthermore, while these three authors describe troublesome geographical and environmental realities, they concurrently employ apocalyptic tropes which appeal to our poetic memory and eschatological anxiety.

Diamond's analysis transcends the geographical and historical; he chooses Shelley's mythic and apocalyptic poem "Ozymandias" as his epigram and shows an aesthetic sensibility and psychological appreciation for Montana. The Bitterroot Valley is "infinitely more beautiful…and peaceful" than Los Angeles, and one of his colleagues remarks that the valley affords a "feeling of tranquility and grandeur."[23] Diamond too feels a sense of eschatological anxiety regarding the West, which he has come to see as a haven and second home. His warning of potential collapse is more ominous when juxtaposed with another chapter on the American West recounting the Anasazi's decline.

I will, therefore, consult an interdisciplinary range of geographical, historical, and mythological studies of the West, in order to gain a greater understanding of the literature itself, as well as to uncover connections with daily life that can become abstracted or lost when examined in a solely artistic light. Richard Slotkin's and Patricia Nelson Limerick's work will supplement Kermode's, Zamora's and Diamond's. Slotkin's comprehensive study of the frontier myth from 1600 through 1992, and Limerick's *Legacy of Conquest* (1987), an overturning of the triumphalist historical narrative in favor of a de-mythologized New Western History, will allow me to consider the *beginnings* of myths compared to the ends Proulx, McCarthy and Alexie explore. Finally, Kermode and Zamora will provide critical bases by which to compare and perhaps judge these Western fictions in the specific terms of eschatology and apocalypse.

What remains of the West according to these authors and the ends they prophesy? Even a reactionary like McCarthy would have to agree that we are no more living in the last days of the biblical Apocalypse now than when John of Patmos had his visions and wrote the book of Revelation almost two millennia ago. As the Gospel writer Mark says, "But about that day or hour no one knows, neither the angels in heaven, nor the Son, but only the Father."[24] Or, to recall a more hostile conception of God, consider Judge Holden's words from *Blood Meridian*, McCarthy's first Western novel, "If God meant to interfere in the degeneracy of mankind would he not have done so by now?"[25]

Consequently, we can examine the aforementioned contemporary fictions and discover in what ways and how they evoke that sense of an ending. We can seek out the various natures and causes of the endings the authors evoke, ask what they want revealed or judged, and why. I hope to gain a wide perspective by researching a white female author, a white male author and a Native American author, each writing about different places and times in the enormous geographical region of the West—Wyoming, the West Texas/Mexico borderlands, and Washington State, respectively. While it is impossible to comment on the entire West, this sampling of authors will afford a greater diversity than would three Texan men, or three Apache women, for example. Conversely, despite radically different backgrounds, perspectives, and political beliefs, all of these authors attack popular Western myths, faulty history, and human arrogance. The common goal is to bring these spurious ideas to an end, and to uncover the reality of the contemporary West beyond that end.

I. From the New World to New Western History and Literature

Often we demonstrate a psychological need to imagine an unknown idyllic place other than where we are. Dissatisfied with our present life, this other place may become a vessel for unfulfilled hopes, personal and cultural. What better place to go than The West? Go West, where the sun sets, fulfill your destiny. Outrun the sun itself, prolong the day, quench your wanderlust in the promised lands on the horizon…

To claim something is ending suggests a critique of the present and of the past, of a mythological or historical beginning. For America, that beginning was 1492. America was, in that age of exploration, invasion and settlement, envisioned as a prelapsarian ideal, a land like that promised to the Israelites. Europeans employed their myth-making apparatus to imagine a fertile New World where history and humanity would flourish. Richard Slotkin's *Regeneration through Violence* (1973), explains how "primary sources from the New World, written by early explorer-conquerors, are couched in the imagery of…romantic European mythology". Columbus's first description of the New World, contains the "traditional imagery of…earthly paradise" which is "generalized, abstracted and vague". Likewise, accounts of Mexico's conquest, written by conquistadores like Cortes, "reflect the strong influence of secular chivalric romances".[1] Lois Parkinson Zamora adds

> To convey to his royal patrons his conviction that his mission represented the fulfillment of apocalyptic prophecy, Columbus referred in letters and in his diary to passages from Revelation and Isaiah which describe the new heaven and new earth. So he immediately initiated what was to become a perennial imaginative association of America with the promise of apocalyptic historical renewal.

Zamora charts the effects of this imaginative association, revealing how Protestants and Catholics believed Revelation might be fulfilled in the New World. The native inhabitants became the lost tribes of Israel; if converted, prophecy would be fulfilled "at once and the kingdom of God might be initiated."[2] If the Indians did not submit to the word of God, they would submit to the sword of God. Hence Slotkin's title—regeneration through violence. Perhaps the European diseases, which devastated the native population far more than any war, were also seen as apocalyptic, divine retribution.

After the explorers and conquerors, many of the first settlers were the seventeenth century Puritans, who sought a particular kind of freedom by journeying West. They wished to build their shining city on a hill; they hoped and prayed that America's virgin territory would hold the "possibility of achieving in the future the primal unity that was lost in the past, when Adam and Eve sinned and were separated from God." Moreover, the "earliest Puritan texts are constant attempts to unite apocalyptic theology and American history: The New World is directly associated with the culmination of history."[3] The minister Cotton Mather, for example, labored to produce a

> ...history of New England 'under the aspect of Eternity'...Puritans and Indians would find their true valuation and be placed in the context of the divine drama of history, as it unfolds from Eden to Calvary to Boston to Apocalypse.[4]

The mythic legacy of this type of history endures. Zamora observes that Christian theology in the New World perpetuated a tradition, which continues to remind us that "Americans on both continents have inherited a sense of the eschatological significance of their historical and national destiny."[5]

This destiny precluded tolerant, peaceful coexistence with the native population. The Puritans' true valuation of the Indians was that of the savage, libidinal other as opposed to the rational, ascetic Anglo. It is partly a reductive and false dichotomy, but it was what many religious leaders insisted upon. This judgment recalls Old World prejudices— the Puritan "horror of Indian myth and ritual [was] derived from the very marrow of its religious tradition. Puritanism began in a revulsion against Catholic and Anglican ritual...against the very idea of blood myths and blood ritual."[6] In America, revulsion at pagan rites resembling Dionysian revels only increased: "the issues were graphically simplified by the racial characters of the pagan antagonists."[7] Furthermore, the land was wild, a blend of "unmitigated harshness and tremendous potential fertility"; Puritans felt a "sense of exile-the psychological anxieties attendant on the tearing up of home roots for wide wandering outward in space and, apparently, backward in time."[8] Richard Etulain likewise comments on the Puritans' psyche: the West outside of the Anglo settlements was, to them, "a howling wilderness, infested with a dark Devil and his minions and barbaric Indians."[9] Thus the horror of the Indian dovetails with an ambivalent Puritan definition of the psychological West. The idea of the New World/West shifted from New Eden to a hellish wilderness, from dream to nightmare, able to accommodate fear and desire.

The Christian versus pagan stereotype solidified into a new American mythology through captivity narratives. Literature originated from instances of Indians capturing settlers; and the concurrent fear of captivity was "ideal" for expressing and resolving spiritual anxiety. This paradigm was "strongly reminiscent of...the fall of man, the apocalypse, and divine judgment" and structurally "reduced a complex series of religious beliefs, philosophical concepts, and historical experiences to a single, compelling, symbolic ritual-drama." A ritual-drama, like Israel's captivity in Babylon and/or Job's suffering, was a test of the soul's worth, offering potential rebirth or "self-transcendence." Ultimately, the Puritan experiences of emigration, conversion, and captivity were "transmuted into myth."[10] Eventually, the hunter/captive myths were enthusiastically invoked during the Indian Wars as an occasion for "imperialistic adventure." Wars were provoked "deliberately and officially...in order to justify the expropriation of Indian lands...The essentially economic basis...was concealed behind a rhetoric which emphasized the need to rescue white captives, particularly women, from the brutal rapists of the plains."[11]

After the seventeenth century, new generations were "more acculturated or acclimated to the wilderness, less like the remembered grandparents in the fixed image of Europe. Exploration of new lands was one necessity imposed upon them; fighting Indians [was another]."[12] Acclimation of newborn Americans, halfway between Frederick Jackson Turner's civilization and savagery, would become quintessential to the national consciousness and mythology. Mountain men, mythic, literary, or real, such as Natty Bumppo, Daniel Boone, and Davey Crocket, exemplified the new national hero. Geographical definitions were also nebulous and caught up in mythology. McMurtry reminds, "historically there have been several Wests," beginning with the Atlantic beaches, then beyond the Cumberland Gap, across the Mississippi, and beyond the 100th Meridian.[13] Where is the West today? Archibald MacLeish might reply, "West is a country in the mind; and so eternal."[14] The frontier moved ever Westward, and there was an increasing "agrarian expansion," similar to those imperialistic adventures, which overlaid a "secular ideology" onto the Christian "eschatological structure of the Frontier Myth."[15]

Secular ideology, and those Enlightenment-influenced intellectuals like Thomas Jefferson who ascribed to it, stood for a paradoxical, de-mythed mythology for the new nation, a progressive mythology aware of itself, liberated from the "dead hand of the past" in the New World.[16] Turner's thesis was a distilled articulation of this supposedly rational, organic frontier mythology. "The Significance of the Frontier in American History" (1893) states:

> American history has been in a large degree the history of the colonization of the Great West. The existence of an area of free land, its

continuous recession, and the advance of American settlement Westward, explain American development...we have...a recurrence of the process of evolution in each Western area reached in the process of expansion...a return to primitive conditions...American social development has been continually beginning over again on the frontier. This perennial rebirth, this fluidity of American life, this expansion Westward with its new opportunities, its continuous touch with the simplicity of primitive society, furnishes the forces dominating American character...[the frontier is the] meeting point between savagery and civilization.[17]

Turner invokes two sociopolitical doctrines of his time: Manifest Destiny and Social Darwinism. His "recurrence of the process of evolution" implies that the white man undergoes a reversion-rebirth: he sheds his latent European/Eastern characteristics in order to become distinctly American, and it is his fate to replace the Indians because of their inherent inferiority and savagery. Turner also links the simplicity of Indian tribal society with primitiveness, though the two are not always causally linked. Finally, although Turner does not speak in religious terms, Slotkin's secular ideology of apocalypse remains, as invocations of "continually beginning over again" and "perennial rebirth" evidence.

Yet the experience of violently colonizing a vast land, and using/exploiting its resources to gain wealth and/or expand the United States' territory was unique for European settlers and immigrants. It instilled in them a sense of nationalism—of entitlement to the land, personal freedom, and financial success—essentially the American Dream. What remains objectionable in Turner's work is his view of Anglo civilization as the pinnacle of civilization itself, and his belief that the land is/was open and free. The latter argument is rather delusional in its blatant elision of the brutality, displacement and genocide of the Indian wars.[18] Slotkin calls the Indian wars, "in many ways the characterizing event of American history."[19] He elaborates on this flawed historiography in *Gunfighter Nation* (1992), offering a different interpretation of Turner's myth of benign but steady progress Westward:

> Violence is central to both the historical development of the Frontier and its mythic representation…the myth of the 'savage war' blames Native Americans as the instigators of a war of extermination…the accusation is better understood as an act of psychological projection that made the Indians scapegoats for the morally troubling side of American expansion.[20]

It is one of the sobering ironies of American history that under the banner of civilization and democracy so many atrocities and blatant injustices occurred.

Another origin of American myth was Buffalo Bill Cody's Wild West Show, which toured the world for almost fifty years, well into the 1930s.[21] The inflated carnival image Cody sold was deliberately and grossly deceitful, but it was popular and lucrative. Many popular notions about the West began with Cody, and their influence has remained potent. Take the example of the thrills, gunfights and womanizing of cowboy life—in reality, he spent up to eighteen hours a day in the saddle and the vast majority of the year on the trail herding cattle. Trips into cowtowns were rare, brief, drunken, and bloody. Still, some cowboys seemed to revel in their "drudgery" and their cowtown escapades, finding "the beat of hardy life in our veins…the glory of work and joy of living."[22] Such an abstracted, positive purview seems more like nostalgic reminiscence caught up in mythmaking than truth. Yet it is in the stark reality of such disparate modes of living that myth takes hold.

Turner declared the frontier closed as of 1890; he viewed the West as completely settled, unable to produce any more economic booms. But there was a uranium frontier/boom in the 1950s, and there has been a methane boom in recent decades.[23] History did not stop; Turner's eschatological invocation was historically and psychologically false. Arguably, the psychological West/frontier took on more importance and became more dominant once there was no more conquerable land.

What of literary beginnings? Most critics agree that James Fenimore Cooper's collection of *Leatherstocking Tales* initiated the paradigms that Western fiction has subsequently worked through. Cooper's variously named hero (Hawkeye, Leatherstocking, Natty Bumppo) has a deliberately indefinite identity. He is the archetypal frontiersman—his independence and self-reliance sacrosanct, his history unnamed, "the complete American of the Myth…who ha[s] defeated and freed himself from both the 'savage' of the Western wilderness and the metropolitan regime of authoritarian politics and class privilege." He "must cross the border into 'Indian country' and experience a 'regression' to a more primitive and natural condition of life so that the false values of the metropolis can be purged, and a new purified social contract enacted."[24] Yet the similarity to Walter Scott's epics of the Scottish Highlands in Cooper's tales calls into question the originality of what aims to be distinctly American literature. Novels like *The Last of the Mohicans* (1826) are patriarchal, Anglo-dominated texts conforming to stereotypes: the Indians are noble savages, and the women are powerless, flat characters. Women are the center over which men struggle to reproduce, but there is also a fear of miscegenation which implies that the Indians are inferior, primitive, and must be supplanted, as the title suggests.

Chief among Cooper's imitators were the nineteenth century dime novelists, who usually eschewed subtleties for excitement, sensationalism, repetitive plots, and elimination of ambiguity in the denouement. Publishers marketed these new, cheap novels to entertain, not educate, and set up a corresponding apparatus of "fiction factor[ies]" with which to cultivate an audience, often consisting of adolescent males or soldiers. In a savvy, sneaky marketing move, publishers often stamped an image of the national currency on their products: "by using the dime itself as their trademark, they fused price and product under the sign of federal authority."[25] This authority implied the construction of something distinctly American—gradually these myths became canonized truths for many readers. Lastly, readers were predominantly Eastern, male, and increasingly urbanized; Eastern writers without any experience of the West published Western books for a voracious Eastern audience seeking an imaginative escape.[26] There was a geographic and thematic disconnection between the apparent authority of the fiction that the authors and the publishers produced and the real history of the West. Instead the mass market fiction of the West became and often remains a blatantly commercial, mythologizing endeavor.

More sophisticated pulp writers such as Owen Wister and Zane Grey replaced the dime Westerns. Grey's famous novel *Riders of the Purple Sage* (1912) explores the struggle between the calming effects of female domesticity and the independent lawlessness of the cowboy. The battle is direr still; it resolves into a question of symbolic castration and a seemingly doomed quest for tangible, satisfying sexual identity. As Scott Emmert notes:

> ...in the stereotypical Western, women often not only play an ancillary role to the adventure tale, but they frequently represent a threat to male independence...the Western becomes a boy's club...its violent milieu is based on 'the sense of decaying masculine potency which has long afflicted American culture.' The six-gun becomes a phallic symbol, and its use represents the symbolic reclamation of a 'masculine supremacy.'[27]

Violence was used with impunity to tame a "savage" West. The hero went West to escape corrupt eastern culture, only to reintroduce a purer, distilled version of that culture once he had found a (castrating) home for himself, if he chose to settle rather than disappear into the horizon with guns blazing and blood flying. Yet there were authors who avoided the myth-making impulse. Mark Twain's *Roughing It* (1872), and Willa Cather's *O Pioneers!* (1913) are good examples, with Twain's characteristic satire and suspicion of all kinds of myth standing alone.

Overall, legend and variously deliberate and innocent historical misunderstanding dominate Western literature from Cooper well into the twentieth century. It was not until the 1960s that literature began to explode these paradigms—Thomas Berger's *Little Big Man* (1964) and Edward Abbey's *Desert Solitaire* (1968) being two excellent examples.

These are the misconceptions and myths which New Western Historians and contemporary Western authors aim to question and revise. They wish to examine the occluded narratives of women and Native Americans, and expose a delusional history written primarily for white men, which simultaneously affects the whole of society. They reject the notion that the West was won through a heroic struggle, and instead maintain it "devastated the environment, ruined much of the land, destroyed the native peoples, penalized minorities, wreaked fiscal havoc…and did in tens of thousands of the would-be winners themselves."[28] Limerick's definition of New Western History in *Trails* (1991)—too long to quote—is apposite; she concludes: "We cannot live responsibly in the American West until we have made a responsible and thorough assessment of our common past."[29] Furthermore, we must acknowledge the complexity and uncertainty of our lives and in the process of recording history. Rather than categorize history into broad, paradoxically limiting compartments, we should be open to multiple perspectives, ready to revise our history, especially if it means trading apparently comfortable myths for painful facts. Accordingly, history and literature become areas of competition for legitimacy

> …to claim…the status of legitimate beneficiary of Western resources… The contest for property and profit has been accompanied by a contest for cultural dominance, struggle over languages, cultures, and religions, the pursuit of legitimacy in a way of life and point of view…this contest remains a primarily unresolved issue of conquest.[30]

Elizabeth Cook-Lynn, in "Why I Can't Read Wallace Stegner" (1996) echoes Limerick: "it may be that Americans will have to…face the loathsome idea that their invasion of the New World was never a movement of moral courage but a pseudo-religious and corrupt socioeconomic movement for the possession of resources…"[31] This assessment of American colonization is perhaps too cynical, especially in its stereotypical dismissal of the whole historical process as a pseudo-religious invasion. But in many cases it is not far from accurate: competition for resources (literal and moral) pervades our lives, our history books, our authors and their characters. It forces us to revise our assumptions about our long-held national myths and those elements that comprise our personal identities.

II. Annie Proulx

Annie Proulx's *Bad Dirt* is determined to critique and discard fraudulent histories, uncover suppressed voices, and knock us down a few pegs on the ontological food chain. The collection is replete with images of decay, sterility and insignificance. As Proulx's title suggests, the land remains infertile, offering no growth or comfort, no place to build or maintain a home. New and old Wyoming residents are stymied in their efforts to achieve tranquility. The land is at best indifferent, at worst malevolent, and humans are portrayed as parasites: it "wanted to go to sand dunes and rattlesnakes, wanted to scrape off its human ticks."[1] Proulx is determined to abolish cozy Western myths—her epigraph quotes serial killer Charlie Starkweather: "They say this is a wonderful world to live in, but I don't believe I ever did really live in a wonderful world."

This collection is less unified than Proulx's first Wyoming Stories, *Close Range* (1999). *Bad Dirt* divides into those stories aligning with Proulx's harsh, disheartening epigram—complex, taut tales which remind of "Brokeback Mountain" and "The Governors of Wyoming"—and those remaining, a "squatting…shadow collection."[2] The former group showcases Proulx's strengths—her "'minute examination of the lives of ordinary people'" and how those people "'conduct their lives in the face of social, economic and ecological change.'"[3] The *TLS* observes that the latter stories "lack [her] high finish and intensity of delivery," they are fanciful but gritty entertainment— burlesque tall tales from the hamlet of Elk Tooth.[4] *The New York Times* argues that these facile stories are "genuinely terrible."[5] To quote Kermode: "fictions too easy we call 'escapist'; we want them not only to console but to make discoveries of the hard truth here and now, in the middest."[6] Perhaps, after documenting the unforgiving, difficult life of contemporary Wyoming, Proulx can only laugh at the "zany antics" of the unimaginative locals who never leave, who take pride in quitting something whenever they please.[7]

Of the remaining stories, Rafferty observes that "'The Indian Wars Refought' and 'The Wamsutter Wolf,' self-immolate in their very last lines, sentences that reduce everything that precedes them to the status of small, dry jokes."[8] The latter story is difficult and disappointing to read. It is difficult because of its unremitting depictions of trailer park squalor—even if this is a true representation of Wyoming life and poverty in apocalyptic contrast to the ideal West, it is employed with a sledgehammer's subtlety and becomes tedious. Furthermore, there is the unsettling feeling that Proulx takes perverse, almost decadent pleasure in relentlessly describing the lives of backward, grime-caked, trailer park denizens. It is disappointing because the story accrues sympathy for its main character Buddy Millar, and also deploys an ominous flaw for him—driving bad dirt back roads which may lead to nowhere or into the teeth of an oncoming storm—only, through a fortuitous concatenation of circumstances, to deliver him from eschatological danger and retreat into macabre fairy tale. The story does self-immolate, casually dispensing poetic justice and taking the metaphorical trope of the alpha wolf controlling the squalid trailer park community too far. Conversely, "The Trickle Down Effect" employs an artistically superior immolation: a drunk driver inadvertently enkindling the hay in the back of his truck with his discarded cigarette butts. Deb Sipple becomes an agent of apocalypse, his "return the closest thing to a meteor shower seen in Elk Tooth, his truck a great fiery cylinder hurtling through the darkness…myriad grass fires…follow[ing] him into town…lay[ing] waste the ranch country."[9] Here something does end with a bang and not a whimper, but most of Proulx's protagonists seem doomed to suffer slowly while their "images of an ideal and seemingly attainable world" dissipate.[10]

In "The Indian Wars Refought," Proulx chronicles the rise and fall of the prominent Brawls family from the "turn of the last century" to the present. Generations of Brawls men were wealthy lawyers, owning a powerful and pristine law office in Casper catering to Buffalo Bill Cody and crooked politicians involved in the Teapot Dome scandal. Now the building is rotting, and when the last male Brawls dies, "ossifi[ied]" in his interests and character, he leaves no children to run his ranch or his law firm. "The Brawls, as the dinosaurs, were gone from Wyoming."[11] The implied white extinction and judicial obsolescence emerges when Sage Brawls' widow Georgina marries Charlie Parrott, part Oglala Sioux.

Proulx sides with the Indians, the Brawls moral authority having turned sour by a lengthy history of corruption and scandal. Alongside the Brawls' imminent disappearance she evokes immanent eschatology—the Brawls' power began in the *fin de siecle* period of the Gilded Age and ended on the "last day of June in 1994." Proulx also dubs the men with gender-bending, anti-cowboy names such as Gay and Vivian, stark and humorous contrasts to their violent masculine surname. Archibald Brawls trades his bad teeth for "dentures that seemed carved from a glacier"—evincing the gap between appearing as durable and strong as a glacier and the fatal reality of smoking induced lung cancer.[12]

The Brawls' decayed law building, with its breached foundation and stinking interior, mirrors the death of the dominant white male and the various Western myths surrounding him. Men have expended their creative and controlling energies and now women and Indians must try to navigate these broken avenues of empowerment. Subsequently, Georgina hires Charlie's daughter Linny to clean out the law building. Linny finds Buffalo Bill's 1913 film re-enacting and praising the Sioux massacre at Wounded Knee as a "wonderful spectacle." First Linny has no idea what happened at Wounded Knee—"they don't teach it in school"—but she researches the past, becomes enraged, and eventually empties the rotting canisters of film onto Georgina's bed before leaving for the reservation. Charlie, though he once felt her indignation, cannot make himself return with her, for he remembers "the awful boredom of the place, the hopeless waiting for nothing."[13]

Is "de-Indianized" Charlie content in the white world? Although he has achieved economic success and sexual fulfillment, "he wanted to get into the nickel misery of those crushed ancestors, measure his schizoid self against the submerged past." Still, he decides not to return; his personal identity and place in contemporary America as an Indian remains haunted by the past and its losses. The past, once unearthed, has enormous power to heal and hurt: hence Rafferty objects to the last line, where Charlie pats his daughter's "unwounded knee."[14] She *is* wounded, psychologically, ensnared in a competition for legitimacy that characterizes an honest confrontation with Western History. That Linny's future and her identity are left in a quandary is something that Proulx seems not to acknowledge in her conclusion, unless we view the utterance "unwounded" as Charlie's perspective and allow Proulx some ironic distance.

Horace Greeley once exhorted young men to Go West and grow up with the country, but the only people going to Wyoming are the old, trying to escape a "choked," "tangled," "drenched in shadow," and "stifling" New England. In "Man Crawling Out of Trees," Mitchell Fair misunderstands from the beginning. He drives West in an "aging Infiniti... 'cutting prairie'...thinking it sounded Western."[15] Later, driving alone, partly trying to escape his wife, he falls prey to a criticism Edward Abbey voiced in Desert Solitaire: "What does accessibility mean? Is there any spot on earth that men have not proved accessible by the simplest means—feet and legs and heart?"[16] Instead of getting out of his car to explore the wilderness, he goes for long drives listening to classical organ music, "experience[ing] the most intense pleasure in being alone." The music reminds him of dinosaurs: "huffing and snorting, [it] smote him…What in the name of god was he listening to?...with shuddering flesh and electric current coursing up his spine he could hardly bear it, the perfect fit of this music to the tawny ground, the abrupt buttes, distant fan of peaks, the monstrous scale of geologic time."[17] While he feels Wyoming's scriptural sublimity (notice how Proulx stamps a religious legacy on his perceptions through the use of the Biblical word *smote*), he fails to experience it directly. From the comfort of his luxury car, Mitchell is caught between two self-simulated, almost cinematic visions of Wyoming's landscape—a primordial Eden and an emotionless Pangaea, the latter of which undercuts his anthropocentrism.

On another drive, he notices a "filthy yellow haze" on the horizon and leaves his truck to ask about the "dust." Proulx's language violently mutates from the esoteric descriptions of the aesthetic beauty Mitchell felt, to the gas station attendant's slang: "Pollution. It's smog. Comes from that goddamn Jonah infill methane gas project…Never seen that smog before in Wyomin. You're seein her start to die. The whoremasters got ahold a her." Mitchell feels full of indignation but takes no action: "There was much more to understanding the place than driving back roads and fitting music to abrupt topography…he was too late…defeated by his ignorance of these most unforgiving, roadless wildernesses." Eventually, his dreams and misconceptions concerning Wyoming's beauty and vigor end—"Everything seemed to end in blood…the wildlife of the place a[nd] the undisturbed country was under assault. Awful diseases were sweeping through the wild creatures… mysterious die-offs teamed with loss of habitat and encroachment on ancient migration routes. He knew he was seeing the end of this wild world and time." For Mitchell it is a bitter and hasty elegy, while Proulx's wider perspective offers an equally brief, but ironic barb, that the land and the Fairs' time in it is "harvested."[18]

His wife Eugenie likewise finds no peace. She would rather be back east designing kitchens, and her unsuccessful attempts to forge new relationships with the locals utterly implode after she becomes too afraid and distrustful to help a "maniac" neighbor crawling through the trees of their backyard with a broken leg.[19] She argues with Mitchell and declares it impossible for her to stay—not that the locals would let them, according to Mitchell. Proulx leaves us with these well-crafted, disturbing words:

> On the plane she looked down on the last of Wyoming, the black mountain ranges capped and splotched with snow, roads like crimped lengths of yarns from unraveled knitting. From on high it seemed human geometry had barely scratched the land. There were few roads, an occasional dammed lake. But most of what lay below was great brown and red curves, scooped cirques, rived canyons with unsteady water in the depths, scalloped rocks whose paler layers resembled lace, eroded slopes that seemed clawed by some monstrous garden tool. On a string-like road below, the few vehicles were the size of pinheads, crawling fleas. Was this was Mitchell saw when he went on those long drives, the diminution of self, a physical reduction to a single gnat isolated from the greater swarm of gnats? The absurdity of living one's life? She thought she would ask him. But of course that did not happen, and any curiosity on the subject was buried under two new ideas—a cowboy kitchen for urban bachelors, and a kind of ranch kitchen with crossed branding irons over the raised hearth to replace the ultramodern German style.[20]

Count the losses: the Fair's unhappy marriage, Mitchell's comforting solitude, and their efforts to integrate into the local community have all failed. The story is the quietly apocalyptic polar opposite of the traditional Easterners' quest West. The title is viscerally frightening, and an image of the evolutionary process which becomes metaphorically thwarted. Rather than an organic, progressive community that shares its resources and life experiences, there is a stark dichotomy between the wealthy, ignorant Easterners and the clannish, poor locals. It is a story about devolution and atomization. Proulx's characters are not nice—they range from fatuous "buffoons" to selfish, afraid, mean-spirited reprobates.[21] Witness Mitchell, the architect, who has failed to build anything. Everything is unraveled, or unraveling.

The land remains—beyond its immediate exploitation, indifferent to human existence. Proulx's final description of Wyoming recalls

"People in Hell Just Want a Drink of Water," from *Close Range*, where she writes "Other cultures have camped here awhile and disappeared. Only earth and sky matter. Only the endlessly repeated flood of morning light. You begin to see that God does not owe us much beyond that."[22] Humbling contemplations of this nature drive the solitary Eugenie into an understated but apparent existential terror. These are the hard truths that Kermode wants from contemporary apocalyptic fiction, and Proulx certainly delivers. Her fear is entirely consonant with our contemporary eschatological anxiety, and Kermode observes that some of the fictional outgrowths of apocalypse have been tragedy, and then existentialism.[23]

For Eugenie, there is nothing beyond this half-thought horror—her unconscious answer to the question she will never ask Mitchell is to retreat into the tangible hyperreality of the commodified kitsch she plans sell to rich Easterners as quintessentially Western. Indeed, some Americans are so desperate for, so entranced with, western mythologies that there is now a market for tumbleweeds, a market worth over $40,000 per year for one Linda Katz.[24] The unnatural kitsch of the manufactured now makes way for the desiccated kitsch of the natural.

What is left of the West? Counterfeit, derivative simulations and images of the Old West to be bought and sold; commodities, rather than individuals, ideals of freedom or community will keep the economy of the New West alive. Although we could argue that from the moment explorers like Columbus encountered the "West" it ceased to exist except as a simulation of itself, in the new millennium, this simulation has been ratcheted up to newfound heights of fraudulence. What is the purpose of Eugenie's life? Make as much money as possible; accumulate as many valuable things as possible; forget your imminent death and insignificance. This is the life philosophy that Eugenie, probably without recognizing it, abides by. When confronted with such a commercialized, nihilistic representation, we must ask whether

Proulx's fiction dramatizes other cultural pursuits or ways of living that offer a more optimistic vision of the future beyond this particular end.

Is Gilbert Wolfscale the only character who receives "the full measure of [Proulx's] love"?[25] She does not idealize him: "he was a model of...stubbornness, savagely possessive of his property... Neighbors said he was self-reliant, but there was a way they said it that meant something else."[26] Gilbert is stubborn, alienated and flawed, not contentedly self-sufficient. His unhappy marriage breaks up; his sons are uninterested in Harp ranch; the country stands against him, metamorphosing from grazing land into desert; his ingenuity is ignored, people want "plastic-wrapped, prebasted Safeway turkeys with breasts like Las Vegas strippers" not homegrown turkeys; and he is "pestered" by "suitcase ranchers," biologists, hunters and environmentalists.[27] He knows the "old world [i]s gone" but he cannot give up his ranch because it evokes his deepest emotions. It reminds him of better, childhood days in the 1950s, when he built a play corral with rock horses. Now, the prairie has "swallowed his horse rocks," those seemingly durable representations of his dreams.[28] He believes Harp is "timeless and unchanging;" he cannot hear its requiem—the "destruction...happened so gradually he had not noticed." Gilbert feels "a strangling love tattooed on his heart," for what was once a beautiful Western idyll has now become a degenerated idol enslaving him.[29]

Through Gilbert's tragedy, Proulx reveals again the "'historical skew between what people have hoped for...who they thought they were, and what befell them.'"[30] The supposed freedom of the West is false, even lethally imprisoning, for today's ranchers. Gilbert recognizes this, if only unconsciously, and he buys a CD called *Remembering Vietnam*, as well as seeking out Vietnam veterans, to tap into a vicarious feeling of danger and excitement. Vietnam was "the great experience of the time of his young manhood and he had been absent."[31] Gilbert, "4-F despite his strength and muscle" longs to have been part of Vietnam because, in a certain twisted way, the *idea* of Vietnam represents everything

Gilbert feels he lacks in his life.³² It would have provided him with potency and purpose rather than a slow, lonesome death— anyone who bothered him he could have, like the gunslingers of old, shot dead instead of being harried by big beef and bleeding-heart environmentalists. Gilbert's vision of Vietnam is a vision of a transplanted psychological West.

After his mother's death, eschatological anxiety creeps into Gilbert himself: civilization begins to "fall away" from him and when he sees his son's thinning hair he feels the "hot breath of passing time." Correspondingly, his ranch disintegrates further—the drought "settl[es] deeper" and poison wastewater from the methane industry seeps into his irrigation ditches. He fights back, going to "strange" meetings where "ecological conservationists and crusty ranchers came together," trying to "keep the old West alive," but the drilling continues.³³ Ultimately, Gilbert despairs, stuck at a red light in his pickup truck, witnessing a parade of mostly obese children dressed in store-bought Wild West attire. The unreal spectacle disillusions him because "there had been no ranchers in the parade—it was all pioneers, outlaws, Indians, and gas." What kind of furniture would Jesus pick?—"he would make the simplest round-legged furniture, everything pegged, no nails or screws."³⁴ Gilbert returns to his ranch alone—old and headed straight to poverty, wishing everything *was* pegged, but knowing it never has, and never will be.

This is Proulx's most sympathetic story, and she is tender to Gilbert, portraying in detail the dreams of his youth and how they have faded away. It is simultaneously her most apocalyptic story, invoking swiftly passing time, the turn of the century, and the ending millennium more than six times, besides the continual barrage of barren images. Moreover, the story explicitly alludes, in its title and in the text, to Jesus' second coming. Gilbert's mother attends a Bible class where people are "tryin to guess how it would be if Jesus showed up."³⁵ But Jesus never does; he is only a shadowy presence in Gilbert's imagination at the story's end. Baudrillard says in *The Illusion of the End* (1994), "it's always the story of Kafka's Messiah: he arrives too late…and the time-lag is unbearable."[36] This is a particularly apt analogy to Gilbert's story. Jesus, if he did come to Wyoming, would be impotent, mute and solitary, not fixing anything, only building simple furniture from "worm-tunneled wood." He would not be the Son of Man presiding over the Last Judgment. The Apocalypse is deferred: "what seemed imminent somehow never came to pass," and Proulx leaves us with poet T. S. Eliot's whimpering end.[37]

III: Cormac McCarthy

No Country for Old Men begins and ends with aging Texas county Sheriff Bell's first-person italicized interchapters. *The Times Literary Supplement* comments, "he thinks the world is getting worse, and yet he also knows that's how old men think."[1] He first tells of a murderer whose execution he attended, who confesses to Bell that he ha d planned to kill somebody "for about as long as he could remember. Said that if they turned him out he'd do it again. Said he knew he was goin to hell...I'd never seen a person like that and it got me wonderin if maybe he was some new kind." Can Bell cope or even communicate with this new kind of killer, who has, by his own admission, no soul? Yet this is nothing compared to what is to come—"somewhere out there is a true and living prophet of destruction and I dont want to confront him...I think a man would have to put his soul at hazard."[2]

Bell is his own non-violent prophet of destruction, his rambling jeremiads set against a breathlessly paced, terse third-person plotline. The New York *Times*, echoing the *TLS*, summarizes his philosophy: "Satan exists, the world is getting worse, and God is too busy with other matters to care. He's written us off and moved on to fresh creations."[3] Later, Bell says "if you were Satan and you were settin around trying to think up somethin that would just bring the human race to its knees what you would probably come up with is narcotics." Bell looks the popular culture in the 1980s and judges it degenerate, violent, profane, uncaring, doomed, and full of dope addicts: "there aint nothin short of the second comin of Christ that can slow this train."[4] He mentions the book of Revelation, as well as Mammon (a Biblical demon personifying greed and materialism) and declares, "I think I know where we're headed. We're bein bought with our own money."[5] We have abandoned God and punishment is due.

There is little immanence in Bell's eschatology—he believes apocalypse is imminent. Furthermore, if his looming eschatology comes true, his world view will be validated, despite his "failure" to stop the novel's murders: "if you got a bad enough dog in your yard people will stay out of it. And they didn't."[6] Gorra argues that Bell's presence is a problem violating McCarthy's artistic strengths—"what remains unclear is the degree to which Bell speaks for the novel as a whole." Bell's warnings of impending doom can become tedious. Gorra suggests "the book seems less fiercely alive on its italicized pages—and the number of these rises sharply as we approach the end."[7] Does Bell therefore speak for the novel, and McCarthy? Vince Brewton proposes that McCarthy, whose early books had an "ambiguous nihilism" haunting them, has now arrived at a "moral destination" that "distinguish[es] clearly between good and evil." Yet while "Good and evil may be clearly distinct...good does not clearly triumph."[8] This is the old is/ought dichotomy. McCarthy dangles his characters' fragile normative dreams before us, and may agree with Bell that we have abandoned God, but he also ruthlessly explores the violent, depraved reality of a God-less society and world where, if God exists, he is indifferent to our degeneracy. Reality is the factual, exterior life of actions, not interior monologue. Gorra observes "it isn't what one thinks that matters, but what one does. And it also makes those doings appear unchosen, unwilled and inevitable."[9]

Enter Anton Chigurh—the book's "monstrous moral centre."[10] He first garrotes one of Sheriff Bell's colleagues—extricating himself from the law "by an act of will"—then steals a car and kills the driver with a pneumatic stungun meant for slaughtering cattle, complete with an air tank.[11] Chigurh "placed his hand on the man's head like a faith healer," and after this chilling sequence we know we have met Bell's prophet of destruction.[12] Chigurh confirms his worst fears—he is a lethal force beyond humanity. Fortunately Bell never confronts Chigurh, because when Chigurh comes into your life, "your life is over." He can never contradict this code because it would make him "vulnerable"; he is the abominable archetype of the Western outlaw.[13]

Reminiscent of Judge Holden, Chigurh epitomizes a fanatical adherence to a Nietzschean will to power through violence. In *Blood Meridian*, Holden orates: "Moral law is an invention of mankind for the disenfranchisement of the powerful in favor of the weak. Historical law subverts it at every turn." From this "historical absolute" Holden tells of a game of chance, of men wagering their lives on the turn of a card, claiming "war is the truest form of divination. It is the testing of one's will and the will of another within the larger will which because it binds them is therefore forced to select. War is the ultimate game because war is at last a forcing of the question of existence. War is god."[14] Chigurh echoes these claims, sometimes employing his game of chance (a coin flip) to flout traditional moral law when confronting his victims. He flips the coin and asks them to call it, to determine whether they will live or die, with the point being that, even if they guess correctly and live, it is by his hand. Their wills cannot match his—he has made them undermine the morals they supposedly adhere to by his very presence and existence, by agreeing to play for the ultimate stakes. He says:

> Most people dont believe there can be such a person. You can see what a problem that must be for them. How to prevail over that which you refuse to acknowledge the existence of. Do you understand? When I came into your life your life was over. It had a beginning, a middle, and an end. This is the end. You can say that things could have turned out differently. That they could have been some other way. But what does that mean? They are not some other way. They are this way. You're asking that I second say the world.[15]

Chigurh is an agent of death, a superhuman harbinger of imminent apocalypse with an implacable claim to authority: life means acting out the will to power, not retreating into imagination or slave morality; life pits man against man—the contest once begun cannot be second-said. The contest/war game is the definitive validation of existence; to deny it is to betray one's life and one's humanity. Therefore both are forfeit; "all punishment is deserved."[16] Or, as Chigurh asks a rival seeker of the stolen drug money: "How does a man decide in what order to abandon his life?"[17] Accordingly, when Chigurh announces "I have no enemies. I dont permit such a thing," he echoes the Judge again: "Whatever in creation exists without my knowledge exists without my consent."[18]

Chigurh enacts his philosophy through his manner of execution; transformed into a cyborg beyond morality, he straps his cattlegun to himself like a symbiotic "prosthesis."[19] Humans are cattle, subject to his will, expendable, weak, prime for slaughter. He tells his last victim: "even a nonbeliever might find it useful to model himself after God."[20] Those who escape his cattlegun he usually shoots in the face, as if their very countenance and brain are offences to him and must be obliterated with extreme violence. He is an intelligent murderer, often engaging his victims in the philosophical arguments above before killing them. He "works" with clinical practice, removing all traces of his existence from a scene (shell casings, etc.) and assiduously caring for his wounds. To Sheriff Bell he becomes a terrible "ghost" that will never be brought to justice.[21] No one is Chigurh's match—Bell never meets him, he dispatches a government agent with ease, and even Llewellyn Moss, the novel's nominal hero and former Vietnam sniper, dies by his hand. His name sounds like *chigger*, the parasite, which is an interesting paradox, implying McCarthy's deep-seated disgust; yet Chigurh's actions simultaneously transcend that judgment. If he is a parasite, he embodies the word's most virulent and fatal manifestation.

That he is part Mexican is another interpretation of Chigurh's "exotically unplaceable" name and obscured origins.[22] He speaks Spanish, and descries a gas station attendant's "cracker view" of things.[23] Such an interpretation dovetails with one of Gorra's major objections— that "the sympathetic characters all have blunt Anglo names" while "the Mexicans don't have any." Furthermore, the Mexican border has a "troubling" symbolic valence which reminds of

"Marlowe's trip upriver in *Heart of Darkness*: a journey into a land beyond law, attractive in its primitivism" but deadly for body and soul, a source of corruption leeching north.[24] Hence Chigurh emerges as a paragon of malevolent, cunning otherness, and likewise into an artistic tradition of European/ Western American characters who have achieved an "evil state of grace."[25] He evokes Conrad's Kurtz, T.S. Eliot's hollow men, Marlon Brando's Kurtz in *Apocalypse Now*, and Judge Holden.[26] This tradition, and the novel itself, inevitably recall "that the disastrous American involvement in Vietnam was the logical conclusion of the ideology of Manifest Destiny."[27] Vietnam was another violent, displaced frontier; it was also, after the two World Wars, widely perceived as the end of the American military's moral authority in the twentieth century. The novel, set in 1980, could be post-apocalyptic, if Vietnam was Apocalypse Now. And perhaps Chigurh's ascendant power began in Vietnam. He bests Moss, an elite fighter, and personally kills his long- time acquaintance Wells, formerly a Special Forces lieutenant colonel in Vietnam.

What of Moss?—he is a noble, heroic fool, devoted to his wife but unable to resist the tempting "false god" of the drug money. He resembles the Border Trilogy's John Grady and Billy Parham in his penchant for quixotic, doomed quests. A stray shot while hunting causes him to stumble on the busted drug deal which begins his anti-Western quest—running for his life through barren desert rather than discovering it on the fertile open range, hiding in motels rather than inhabiting the harsh, beautiful landscape. Much of this novel's action is spent sequestered *inside* dark hotel rooms, claustrophobically peering *outside* between curtains. When Moss meets Chigurh, Chigurh is "beyond Moss's experience," as his transient, benign surname suggests.[28]

Llewelyn is a Welsh-Gaelic name, which returns us to Yeats' poem. McCarthy's allusion reads:

> Moss walked out onto the prairie behind the motel with one of the motel pillows under his arm and he wrapped the pillow around the muzzle of the gun and fired off three rounds and then stood there in the cold sunlight watching the feathers drift across the gray chaparral, thinking about his life, what was past and what was to come.[29]

McCarthy turns Yeats's mythic poem against itself. Moss is not going to be gathered into the artifice of eternity as a golden bird—feathers here are decidedly ephemeral, destroyed by his gun. God's holy fire is absent; there is only cold sunlight. Moss's impulsive quest into the mythic West has set sail to nowhere but a violent death without dignity or transcendence. It is a death-haunted book—there are no young in one another's arms and the marriages produce no children. The West is no country for young men, let alone a paltry, aged man like Sheriff Bell, who tangentially recalls Yeats again when he says "we are all of us ill-prepared for what is to come." He knows he has been "beaten" by Chigurh and the feeling is "more bitter to him than death." He attempts to endure however, telling himself "you need to get over that." Accordingly, Bell has a curious dream at the novel's end: his father rides past him on a horse "carryin fire in a horn the way people used to do and I could see the horn from the light inside of it. About the color of the moon. And in the dream I knew that he was goin on ahead and that he was fixin to make a fire somewhere out there in all that dark and all that cold."[30] Arguably, the novel ends with a dream of Yeats' holy fire of re-creation, opposed to its beginning with an execution. Still, the is/ought problem remains, and it seems a meager hope that Bell's dream balances out this apocalyptic novel's pervading sense of judgment and death. Bell only survives because he has not met Chigurh. Chigurh's is the way of the future, and "that God lives in silence who has scoured the following land with salt and ash."[31] We are already defeated, soon to be extinct.

By the end of *No Country for Old Men*, McCarthy achieves a totality of his apocalyptic vision. He presents a figurative cataclysm and sets the stage for corresponding moral and cultural endings. It is not surprising, then, that McCarthy's most recent and more acclaimed novel, *The Road* (2006), is a stark immediate tale of a father and son trying to survive in a near-future earth razed by nuclear holocaust. The narrative is stripped down to the barest essentials of survival and human emotion, to the point that there is not only an apocalypse of form—a sense that McCarthy is dismantling the notion of narrative itself—but of mythology, anthropocentrism, characters, even our basic language apparatus for understanding the world: "The sacred idiom shorn of its referents and so of its reality."[32]

Some few people have survived, and this brings McCarthy's perennial question of human nature more acutely to the fore. How would humans treat each other in such a situation? Would there be a renovation, a new beginning, or would there be that final degeneration into animal brutality? The potential apocalypse of the human emotional core, the extinguishing of the fire (McCarthy uses the same image repeatedly in the novel), the cauterization of compassionate morality—this, in turn, is what is at stake in *The Road*.

Seen in this light, *The Road* follows naturally on the heels of *No Country*, and together these two novels are the logical conclusion to a life's work, an apocalypse of the author himself. Indeed, it will be surprising to see if Cormac McCarthy publishes any more fiction in his lifetime and, if so, what story he will possibly have left to tell. With *Suttree* (1979) he wrote himself out of Appalachia, and now he has written himself out of the West. To be accurate, he has written himself out of recorded time.

IV: Sherman Alexie

In *The Lone Ranger...*, Sherman Alexie's primary concern is the potential end of the tribe. How do Indians preserve their tribal history? Who among them wants to preserve that heartbreaking history? How do they escape the poverty, dead-end alcoholism, lack of ambition, and lack of role models inhabiting the reservation? "We wear fear now like a turquoise choker, like a familiar shawl," Alexie's alter-ego Victor says.[1] There is a crucial tension between movement and stasis—Indians must move on from their petrified apocalypse, where young Indian men become feminized and neutered, paralyzed on the reservation, "wrapped in shawls,"[2] mythologizing fallen heroes, and crying "the same old Indian tears."[3]

Alexie recalls the concrete, painful historical legacy of the Indian Wars. When his characters comment that they are suspicious of "forced movement," where a white character would simply seem neurotic, this carries profound historical resonances.[4] White people are not in such dire danger of disappearance. These moments recall the broken treaties, the Trail of Tears, and the Indians' confinement onto the reservations, the "white man's prisons to get the Indians off the good land."[5]

There is also a danger of assuming, like Turner, that the Indians were on the wane, always stuck and poverty-stricken on small bits of land, that Anglo-Saxons were simply moving into places that the Indians had previously, conveniently vacated. This kind of historical forgetfulness, according to Alexie, can precipitate disappearance: "I know somebody must be thinking about us because if they weren't we'd just disappear just like those Indians who used to climb the pueblos."[6] Cook-Lynn elaborates: "the declaration of Indian demise has done much harm…concepts of indigenousness and aboriginality are mis-defined and misunderstood by the reading public…" This old stereotype may deprive the Indians of a coherent identity, and worse, nostalgically refers to them as prehistoric.[7]

Alexie's above invocation of the Anasazi is a key referent throughout much of Western fiction. It has become somewhat obligatory to have an Anasazi moment in one's book. Proulx's "Dump Junk," a *Bad Dirt* story featuring concurrent themes of disappearance and petrifaction, says: "the cliff dwellers must have been the most agile of human beings."[8] In *Blood Meridian*, the Judge says:

> They quit these parts, routed by drought or disease or by wandering bands of marauders, quit these parts ages since and of them there is no memory. They are rumors and ghosts in this land and much revered. The tools, the art, the building—these things stand in judgment on the latter races...All progressions from a higher to a lower order are marked by ruins and mystery and a residue of nameless rage. So. Here are the dead fathers. Their spirit lies entombed in the stone. It lies upon the land with the same weight and ubiquity. For whoever makes a shelter of reeds and hides has joined his spirit to the common destiny of creatures and he will subside back into the primal mud with scarcely a cry. But who builds in stone seeks to alter the structure of the universe and so it was with these masons however primitive their works may seem to us.[9]

The Judge's mesmerizing words reveal a fundamental paradox—our love and terror of disappeared high culture, whether it be Anasazi, Mayan, Greek, Roman, or another. Confronting the cliff dwellers' ruins tickles a morbid curiosity in us; we feel a tension between discovery of and nostalgia for what has ended, and the suddenly imminent possibility of a cultural apocalypse. Our eschatological anxiety is at once consoled and inflamed.

In Alexie's fiction, his characters fear that people and history itself will forget them, that they will subsequently disappear like the Old Ones, "with food still cooking in the pot and air waiting to be breathed...they turned into birds or dust or the blue of the sky or the yellow of the sun."[10] Alexie refutes this possibility through his constant reference to the past, though most of his stories are set in the near present. He believes the past is still relevant, but the cataclysmic relocation and reduction of the Indian people has left him with an antipathetic outlook towards America and lacking a concept of homeland. In response to the question of genocide, Alexie has said:

> That is the Aboriginal Sin of this country...it will never be part of the national conversation. To do so would shake the very foundations of the country. To admit responsibility for that—then they would have to honor the treaties...All governments are sociopathic. They're serial killers...and have the methodology of serial killers. Serial killers always think they're right.
> *How come you're not angrier?*
> Then you die. I don't believe in people I guess...I don't get disappointed. I think in the end most people have faith in human beings. I don't...when people are good, including myself, I'm surprised and pleased by it...
> *That's very cynical.*
> I'm Indian [laughs]. How could you not be cynical? I think it's optimism that gets you in trouble...I try to write with imagination about a real world. A world in which I grew up, the world in which I live now.[11]

Injustices continue—in that world in which Alexie grew up, in the 1970s, the Indian Health Services sterilized many Indian women without their consent.[12] Spokanes are still a "dispossessed, subaltern people."[13] The constant movement between past and present, with both states of being confused and painful, lends a kind of schizophrenic effect to his short story collection. Constant movement and questioning of history also work in the revealing, uncovering spirit of apocalypse that Zamora defines, exposing the "'Ironies of Anglo-Indian relations.'"[14] Alexie's simultaneously bleak, hopeful and humorous outlook permeates his stories. It is often humor, the "antiseptic that cleaned the deepest of personal wounds," that combats injustices and absurdities, allowing Alexie's Indians to survive.[15]

The title story, however is not very humorous. It presents the insomniac narrator, living in Seattle with his white girlfriend, and portrays an intense feeling of dislocation and alienation, or the "solitary confinement" of Kermode's existential apocalypse.[16] His relationship with his girlfriend is difficult and eventually fails; he repeatedly breaks lamps when they fight, as if the darkness could erase their ethnic difference. Doubtless he feels like another of Alexie's male characters: "[I] kissed the white girl, I felt the good-byes I was saying to my entire tribe." He expands this microcosmic relationship, through a recurring nightmare, into the whole history of white and red, where the three white soldiers play polo with a dead Indian woman's head. The narrator's iconoclastic refusal to assimilate into white culture leads to both metaphorical paralysis and aimless wandering, verging on the breakdown of the self. "I knew there were plenty of places I wanted to be, but none where I was supposed to be," he tells us, and later on, when he is pulled over for driving through a white neighborhood by a policeman, he thinks, "I wanted to tell him I didn't really fit the profile of the country, but I knew it would just get me into trouble."[17]

The story also contains an insight into our eschatology. The narrator picks up a "week-old" newspaper reporting "another civil war, another terrorist bomb exploded, one more plane crashed and all aboard were presumed dead. The crime rate was rising in every city…and a farmer in Iowa shot his banker" and juxtaposes it with "a kid from Spokane won the local spelling bee by spelling the word *rhinoceros*."[18] The apocalypse is deferred again, if not rendered false; the world is going to hell as usual, a week ago, and is simultaneously able to sustain small, humble successes (the spelling bee winner) as opposed to grandiose destruction and tragedy. Conversely, this passage confirms Alexie's fear of disappearance—the newspaper makes no mention of Indians. As Kermode says, "Apocalypse can be disconfirmed without being discredited."[19]

Where is the narrator to go? He returns "home" to the reservation for a time, for "Indians can reside in the city but they can never live there." Yet this is an unfulfilling return, engendering further ennui. He also finds himself bested by a white basketball player, a particularly galling defeat because basketball is such an important Spokane reservation pastime. Furthermore, as the narrator is college-educated he is expected to achieve more; he is the "new kind of warrior," but he has an uncertain conception of himself and how he is to fight, and his battles bring few, if any, victories. At the end, his white ex-girlfriend says "I want to change the world."[20] This recalls that positive-normative tension, to which we have already heard one chilling reply—*you cannot secondsay the world.*

Alexie sets imagination and, ultimately, storytelling, against Chigurh's claim. "Imagining the Reservation," presents evocative, apocalyptic imagery and an imperative call to arms: Imagine. He envisions an alternate American history: "Imagine crazy horse invented the atom bomb in 1876 and detonated it over Washington D.C.... Imagine Columbus landed in 1492 and some tribe or another drowned him in the ocean."[21] This is a startling way of simultaneously attacking historical sacred cows, of hoping for a better, humbler future which acknowledges past errors, and of creating a "wish-fulfilling narrative... [that] renews a sense of [historical] tragedy."[22] These interconnected tensions cohere on the reservation, both a prison and a sanctuary. The Indians face a Catch-22: if they remain on the reservation they will have cultural continuity, but within a circumscribed, barren and uranium-polluted space with few opportunities; if they leave they are divorced from their heritage but may find economic success.[23] Neil Campbell observes that, in Alexie's fiction, "there is no easy route back to ceremony or to the land that heals."[24] Indians might also become trapped in the "cable television reservation" in the white world, where disappearance and assimilation are realities. The American Melting Pot is annihilation; the fractions will take over. Alexie says, "Survival = Anger X Imagination," since imagination is "the only weapon on the reservation."[25]

Alexie sees the reservation as a place of latent creative potential.[26] If other Indians like himself can be educated, yet remain connected with their tribal roots, Indian culture could have a renaissance. Conversely,

"How can we imagine a new language when the language of the enemy keeps our dismembered tongues tied to his belt?" Adrian wants to "rasp into sober cryptology and say something dynamic" but he cannot because it is his laundry night—again reflecting the stifling social slavery that the Indians still feel. Call it a conflict between nation and narration, or a competition for legitimacy—for Indians July 4th is not Independence Day, instead, "all is Hell."[27]

Still, Alexie never loses hope in the power of imagination. He remembers using food colorings on the potatoes he ate every day as a child, a simple act of redemption that insured survival. Imagination even allows him to contemplate forgiveness. In the closing sentences, the diction is important. Alexie asks us to imagine "an escape," that your shadow is "a perfect door," a "song" a "spring [of water]" a "drum," and "a story that puts wood in the fireplace."[28] He presents his philosophy in miniature, imagining potent, peaceful and natural things apart from the commodified white world that resonate with the reader. Ultimately, what puts wood in the fireplace, promising survival?—a good story.

That is the theme of Alexie's deceptively simple story by the same name. It is an explicit, metafictional dramatization of the process of survival that is implicit in all the other stories. The tripartite story begins with the narrator's mother quilting, a communal activity that she does alone. When she asks the narrator to tell a good story, since "people should know that good things always happen to Indians too," the narrator says, "If you want to hear a good story you have to listen," and it is clear that he is not only speaking to his mother, but to us, to his people, to the world. Then he remembers the deceased Uncle Moses, whose house is "held up by the tribal imagination." The name recalls the archetypal Biblical leader and prophet who freed the enslaved Israelites and introduced basic moral and democratic law. Moses is, in both stories, an agent of apocalyptic change. Moses holds his last bite of food in his mouth "like the last word of a good story"—an ingenious metaphor that ties storytelling into life-giving and food into imagination and survival.[29] Then a young boy runs up to Uncle Moses, skipping a basketball trip, because he wanted to see the old man. This is the good thing: the boy wanting to learn about his heritage from Moses, and it gains more resonance when one remembers the context surrounding basketball on the reservation. Where basketball stars fail and succumb to alcoholism, the apparently simple choice Arnold has made becomes wise, almost prophetic, again insuring survival. A good story functions on many different levels—it allows for a re-telling of history, for a survival and expansion of tribal imagination, for a way to put food on the table, and for a way to resist Hollywood visions.

This hopeful message stands in contrast to most other forms of storytelling in the collection. Andrew Dix argues that many of Alexie's characters wish to escape from stories, not into them.[30] Indians are "situated at a boundary between cultural rejection and cultural connection."[31] Thomas-Builds-the-Fire, the reservation storyteller, is often persecuted or ignored. Indians are suspicious of him, tired of being reminded of their catastrophic losses, want to, like Stephen Daedalus, wake up from the nightmare of history. It is for this reason that Alexie titles one of his stories "A Drug Called Tradition," the image suggesting that tradition is euphoric, but also "artificial" addictive and debilitating.[32] Characters are reluctant to move forward, to "keep moving, keep walking, in step with [their] skeletons," and Alexie shows an implicit impatience with his tribe for not being more ambitious and dedicated to improving their situation: "sometimes it seems like all Indians can do is talk about the disappeared."[33] Yet "an unsparing examination of what is gone and what remains," like Yeats' golden bird singing of what is past, passing and to come, teaches survival.[34] Ultimately, Alexie's mature characters align themselves with Thomas' point of view; stories can change the world.

Conclusion: Beyond Apocalypse— Western Places and Myths in the 21st Century

The West is dead; long live the West. As Zamora writes, when it comes to apocalypse, "there are no last words on the subject."[1] We are still in *medias res*, and despite parts of the West's dilapidation, the myths especially endure, metamorphose, continue to delude and inspire. McMurtry contends

> ...there is still the West that was—with its achievement and its destruction—and the land that is, emptier and emptier on the plains, more and more weighed down with population on the Gulf and West Coasts, and, always, that other, endlessly imagined West, the West that can never be fully believed or wholly denied.[2]

The continued, if not increased, popularity of Western merchandise and art attest to this phenomenon. The frontier is especially alive and well in science fiction and fantasy. From Edgar Rice Burroughs' eugenics-laden Mars and Tarzan novels, to *Star Trek*, to Stephen *King's Dark Tower* books, the West thrives in popular culture. Turner's thesis and its subsequent cultural exponents may be down for the count in academia, but have been wholly inscribed into the popular, imagined West. This is something "accurate scholarship can't do a thing about" because the imagination has "a potency with the public that modest truths can rarely match." Still, "honest scholars and serious writers grit their teeth and soldier on;" they may take comfort in the high amount of quality Western scholarship coming out of many universities in the past few decades, and in the fame of authors such as Proulx, McCarthy and Alexie, who undoubtedly reach a greater audience than the academics.[3] Some of this work is bound to break through cultural assumptions and cause people to question them. Regardless, the intense interest in and debate over the West speak to the fact that

> In American popular culture the West is still seen as inviting and special, as a place where people should be stronger and freer... To the extent that the West is still seen as a place where our national character is formed and tested, it becomes an ideal setting for writers and filmmakers who wish to provoke an examination of issues that overlay the question of who Americans are and who they are becoming.[4]

McCarthy's move to this ideal setting, from his native Tennessee to West Texas, took him from near-poverty and obscurity to financial success and international acclaim. The quality of his fiction has always been of a high caliber, but it is the Western context, that crucible which tests and forges the American identity, which has struck such a chord with critics and audiences alike. As he has said, "there isn't a place in the world you can go where they don't know about cowboys and Indians and the myth of the West."[5] McCarthy's recognition of the myth's worldwide pervasiveness, and the metaphysical/philosophical concerns his fiction raises, reveals his interest in questions of human nature in addition to the question of who Americans are and who they are becoming. His Western fictions contain apocalyptic moments and themes which "react against the old system," in this case the myths of the old West.[6] Against Turner's progressive, bloodless and benign winning of the West, McCarthy gave us *Blood Meridian*. His indictment of humanity there is comprehensive—one of the epigrams quotes the *Yuma Daily Sun*: "...a re-examination of a 300,000 year old fossil skull found in the same region [of Ethiopia] earlier shows evidence of having been scalped." Killing with impunity and vicious bloodlust is innate to all of humanity for all of history; neither whites nor Hispanics, nor Indians are exempt from this brutal reality. McCarthy sharply questions our notions of progress and democratic humanism. He argues:

> There's no such thing as a life without bloodshed...I think the notion that the species can be improved in some way, that everyone should live in harmony, is really a dangerous idea. Those who are afflicted with this notion are the first

ones to give up their souls, their freedom. Your desire that it be that way will enslave you and make your life vacuous.[7]

McCarthy's philosophy is elusive, but he seems to have little use for normative ends and their advocacy, as the repetitive failure of his heroes suggests. His work entertains desire and democracy, but continually conceives of the former as crippling and the latter as unnatural to human nature. Michiko Kakutani muses that Chigurh adheres to an "ancient Hobbesian code of war," and there is a crucial tension between the allure of McCarthy's violent villains and their undeniable monstrosity, their callous inhumanity.[8] Hobbes does invite parallels to McCarthy's work, in the disparity between characters like Chigurh and the Judge, and McCarthy himself. These characters revel in Hobbes's nasty, brutish and short state of nature, in man's inhumanity to man, finding in it the Nietzschean will to power. Hence, war is god. Conversely, McCarthy appears one step removed from this conclusion, and it is unclear whether he would, like Hobbes, wish for a Leviathan which would keep violence and injustice in check. Such a conclusion seems like an enslaving desire, another false god.

Foucault once wrote of Nietzsche's genealogical process of morality, "Humanity does not gradually progress from combat to combat until it arrives at universal reciprocity, where the rule of law finally replaces warfare; humanity installs each of its violences in a system of rules and thus proceeds from domination to domination."[9] McCarthy seems keenly interested in documenting yet disagreeing with Foucault's process of domination, this Nietzschean will to power and violence valued as a positive and natural force of becoming. Still, his disagreement has a kind of fatalism inscribed into it—the species cannot be improved; dreams tend to fail. Gorra argues McCarthy has "an odd resemblance to the high Modernists" who longed for a new kind of certainty, built out of the Great War's apocalyptic rubble.[10] Accordingly, McCarthy may remind of Yeats, but his implicit dismantling of Yeats' poem in *No Country for Old Men* and Bell's Christian beliefs suggests he better resembles T. S. Eliot, a reactionary whose sentiments aligned with an existential Christianity, not Yeats' Nietzschean, warmongering fascism.

Chigurh believes you cannot secondsay the world, yet the act of writing is precisely such a counter-narrative. For all McCarthy's violence and talk of war being God, critics have argued that his Western novels contain an underlying protest against these very things. Though *Blood Meridian's* perspectives remain much wider (it is more aptly described as a retelling of *Moby-Dick* than anything else), it may also be read as a retelling and critique of Vietnam.[11] Likewise, the Border Trilogy shows "significant traces" of the "imaginative legacy of the 1991 Gulf War."[12] *No Country for Old Men* is the first McCarthy novel explicitly dealing with Vietnam's controversial legacy, and there is a sense that the cat is at last out of the proverbial bag when one of the characters says, "you can't go to war like that."[13]

Again, foreign wars represent a transplanted, transmuted West. Slotkin argues that the frontier myth periodically loses its credibility in the national consciousness, yet undergoes a "recrudescence" during election campaigns and wars. President Johnson invoked the "characteristic imagery of the captivity myth" on behalf of "escalating the war in Vietnam" in 1965.[14] We have since gone to war against Afghanistan, and twice against Iraq, with similar logic underpinning our decision—to free an oppressed people and bring law to a lawless land. The complicated valence of September 11, 2001, with its own apocalyptic moment and subsequent recrudescent mythology of martyrdom, just punishment and revenge, has contributed to the urgency and sense of purpose behind the subsequent invasions of Afghanistan and Iraq. Soldiers are modern-day cowboys: international news reports tell of vigilante Americans and independent security companies like Blackwater styling themselves as "Kabul's Colonel Kurtz," and of the wild Western provinces of Iraq, where twenty-first century gunslingers hunt down insurgents.[15] The media remains habitually complicit with this lurid, reborn cowboy brutality, selling a stylized simulacrum of the world's war and violence to us on the TV as part and parcel of the carnival that is Baudrillard's hyperreal America. The news itself is commodified infotainment, often more concerned with ratings and popularity than reportage as such.

Ultimately, frontier metaphors continue to permeate our cultural consciousness, serving as shorthand for our dreams of freedom, power, vengeance and renewal. Literature like McCarthy's offers a contrasting voice to both past and present embodiments of these Western myths. Even Sheriff Bell admits to the ambiguity of life in the West and the difficulty of achieving incontrovertible truth: "It's a life's work to see yourself for what you are and even then you might be wrong."[16] As Neil Campbell writes, "the New West [i]s an unfinished, unfinishable story constantly awaiting new narratives."[17] This statement is at once conveniently and painfully true, buying into both the roseate mythological notion of the West as endlessly renewing and renewable, and revealing, perhaps in spite of itself, that barring nuclear holocaust, there will always be some story that can be told about the West, no matter its state of health or dilapidation.

We might set a recent news story against Proulx's down-and-out, drought-ridden depiction of ranch life. In 2007, Texas A&M opened an Institute for Ranch Management, which offers MBAs to young ranchers willing to learn about "rangeland specialties, including animal nutrition and wildlife management."[18] To what degree this educational endeavor will be reinscribed back into the exploitative system of late capitalism, versus manifesting a tangible appreciation for the individual landowner, an alternative to mere commodification of a bankrupt mythology, and a responsible environmental attitude, remains to be seen. Regardless, it is an interesting development for the West, and does present an opportunity for new narratives.

Are there any new narratives awaiting Annie Proulx in Wyoming? Rafferty wonders whether the artistic inspiration Proulx once felt there has ended in "imaginative drought. When you look at the West and all you can see are the wide open spaces between people's ears, it's time to hit the trail."[19] Born in New England, Proulx said when she first settled in Wyoming that its "'long sight-lines encourage clarity of vision…the roll of high planes and stony steeps satisfy some inner longings smothered by my native New England woods.'"[20] The aesthetic beauty of the West may be all that Proulx has left—if so, it is a lonely and solitary end to her paradigmatic Western journey as an artist. Unlike the down and out people she portrays, she has the money and wherewithal to leave whenever she pleases.

As a narrator, Proulx seems impatient with her flawed, narrow-minded characters. This, along with the more overt apocalyptic themes we have discussed, represent an important shift from the more languorous and appreciative glance she cast on Wyoming in *Close Range*. If nothing else, her dire predictions for the future call our attention to her concerns in a more direct, if not effective, manner. While in 2004 it seemed that she was finished writing about Wyoming, this was not the case: she published her third collection of Wyoming stories, entitled *Fine Just the Way It Is*, in late 2008. Time will tell whether there are indeed new and relevant narratives for her beyond bad dirt back roads and the downward ranching spiral, but it takes little time for the reader to notice that the title of her third collection is a stubborn and satirical one, not a reference to rehabilitation or rebirth.

For now, Proulx's Wyoming remains on the brink of ecological and mythic collapse. Like Mitchell and Eugenie's marriage spoiled by the "snake enter[ing] the garden," Wyoming offers little freedom, only imprisonment, pollution, existential insignificance, and death.[21] It is a vision of America's heartland decimated, extinct, and plundered. Proulx's work, like Diamond's, stands as a hard warning about the consequences of misused and wasted natural resources. Those surviving are mired in poverty, alcoholism, bestiality, and drug addiction. Like Governor Emerson from *Close Range*, "past his apogee and falling,"[22] the metaphorical woodsman's axe in Bad Dirt has reached the "apogee of the swing and…beg[un] its irrevocable descent."[23]

Irrevocable descent leads into tragedy and negative existentialism in several of Proulx's stories. Gilbert Wolfscale's story is like the "broken apocalypse" of King Lear, a "terrible farce," but the existential dilemma is more troublesome.[24] Faced with the absurdity of living one's life, we wonder if Eugenie speaks for Proulx. Eugenie cannot conceive of a liberating existentialism like that kind Edward Abbey found in *Desert Solitaire*—she "experiences an 'absurd' world without secure 'foundations': [s]he is therefore thrown back upon [her]self as the source of values and meanings," but inside herself there is nothing but a scheme to cash in on the West's commercial potential. That Proulx does not show any main characters accepting this doctrine of "radical freedom and responsibility" does not necessarily mean that she believes as Eugenie does.[25] Rather, that Proulx bothers to write such an elegiac collection reveals a passionate soul mourning Wyoming's hard times and protesting through her art in order to affect apocalyptic change, to wake us up if we happen to be in a Eugenie-like nihilistic slumber.

Proulx's distaste for Eugenie as a character, along with the hyper-real parade Gilbert must witness, recalls an earlier condemnation of contemporary American culture. Baudrillard writes in *America* (1988): "The microwave, the waste disposal, the orgasmic electricity of the carpets: this soft, resort-style civilization irresistibly evokes the end of the world."[26] This version of America is raised on processed food and poisoned water; it is fat, fed on decadent Las Vegas dreams. Sucking up streams and lakes and rivers to grow grass in the Arizona desert. In this version of America, history is irrelevant and forgotten, and we are a nation of amnesiacs, our greedy hands grabbing all the money they can. Communion is a bucket of KFC ordered from a machine.

Obviously this is not America in its entirety; America is anything but a monolithic entity—but this bloated, wasteful and hyper-real component remains a large part of our national identity. While the 2008 Presidential election and concurrent severe contraction of global financial markets may indicate a cultural shift away from this worldview, it remains to be seen whether significant change will occur within the political, ideological, and cultural spheres. In the meantime, it is this cynical debauched culture that the United States so often exports to the rest of the world. Saul Bellow has said, "'This society, like decadent Rome, is an amusement society. That is the grim fact.'" The artist must be a "prophet," set against such a society. In this case, it becomes imperative that the artist secondsay the world, and "propose a means of continuing to live in our time."[27] On the surface, Proulx's text remains largely silent on this question; there is no Monkey Wrench Gang cavorting around Wyoming towns culture-jamming the various myths we have identified as malaises. This is better than a political screed—Proulx allows us to contemplate her unflinching portrayal of the sorrow and squalor of her characters and arrive at our own conclusions. Implicitly, however, her apocalyptic invocations and repulsive characters act as a kind of collective prophecy. Proulx sets herself against the arrogant smash-and-grab instant gratification that consumer culture promises, and while she may not overtly propose a means of continuing to live in the West, she certainly suggests how not to live.

Perhaps the movement toward a sustainable future begins with what Michael L. Johnson, in his 2007 book of criticism on Western Literature and culture *Hunger for the Wild*, calls an "atonement of nature and culture."[28] Perhaps that is yet another arrogant humanist delusion that McCarthy would denounce. Personally, I would like to believe that a humble attempt at such atonement would not enslave us and make our lives vacuous. Rather, that it might offer the possibility of appreciating and preserving the abundance we still enjoy, and encourage us to try to rebuild those things that we have knowingly and unknowingly destroyed. As McCarthy himself wrote in *The Crossing* (1993), "like every man who comes to the end of something, there was nothing to be done but to begin again."[29]

What is certain is that writer-artist must, as humbly and truthfully as they can, take up challenge of being a prophet. The writers must write their stories and reveal to us that which we remain blind to; the reader must read and think deeply about these revelations. In so doing, we allow for what Homi Bhaba calls "counter-narratives" to enter the discourse of power relations and ideology: we allow for the "renegotiation of those times, terms, and traditions through which we turn our uncertain, passing contemporaneity into the signs of history."[30]

For Sherman Alexie, storytelling was Bellow's means of empowerment, allowing him to escape both alcoholism and the reservation. He now believes that it is possible for Indians to live and survive in the city, and wants to write about the over 60% of Indians who live in urban areas.[31] If anything, his trenchant irony has increased; he has hardly become assimilated into white culture. His most recent collection of short stories, *Ten Little Indians* (2003), takes aim at the attacks on the World Trade Center, among other things. Calling the media circus following 9/11 into question, he writes, "it was awful and obscene, all of it, it was grief porn," before asking "Don't you think there was at least one man in the towers who deserved to die?"[32] Besides questioning the officially sanctioned meanings of the event, Alexie's challenges reveal the possibility that the "concept of crisis it itself in crisis."[33] Likewise, Kermode observes that history and eschatology can become the same thing—every moment is a crisis.[34] In such a situation, one must strive to be more than a "doomsayer," one must acknowledge that life will go on, ask difficult questions, and strive to understand history's message.[35] Accordingly, Alexie has also continued to confront the hypocrisy he sees in American culture. When asked if Indian gaming is immoral, he replied, "Not any more than selling tobacco. Capitalism by definition is the exploitation of vice. My bothers and sisters work in the bingo halls because they want to feed their families."[36] In my home state of New York, Indian tribes are using some of the money gained from mostly white gamblers to buy back ancestral lands. Ironically, this decadent, amusement society is being bought with its own money, as Sheriff Bell might say.

Socrates once famously declared that the unexamined life is not worth living, an apocalyptic statement entirely commensurate with these three authors and their conceptions of the normative possibilities held within the contemporary West. It is ultimately a question of humility, of the process of becoming as human beings. Neil Campbell argues that Alexie's work is Bakhtinian, full of a "dialogical culture of negation/affirmation and symboliz[ing] identity as mobile, about becoming not being."[37] In a similar spirit, Proulx and McCarthy question much of Western history and rarely allow one character or mouthpiece to dominate the text. This multiplicity of perspectives and ontological revaluation of myths is the natural result of a healthy competition for legitimacy—it allows Linny to discover her lost heritage, for us to recognize Moss's odd, failed quest as still resembling the paradigmatic Western quest, and for us to apprehend the humorous, yet serious tension in Alexie's image of the Lone Ranger and Tonto fistfighting. Kermode says, "those books which seal off the long perspectives, which sever us from our losses…these are the books which, when the drug wears off, go on to the dump with the other empty bottles."[38] Here, in these Western fictions, we have found something different, something which is at once humbling and empowering. As Sherman Alexie once asked the audience at a lecture I attended—*live your life as though you could be wrong.*

Notes

Introduction: Apocalypse and The Contemporary West

[1] Zamora, Lois Parkinson. *Writing the Apocalypse: Historical Vision in Contemporary U.S. and Latin American Fiction.* (Cambridge: Cambridge U.P., 1989), p. 1.
[2] McMurtry, Larry. *Sacagawea's Nickname: Essays on the American West.* (New York: New York Review of Books, 2001), p. 9.
[3] Kermode, Frank. *The Sense of an Ending: Studies in the Theory of Fiction.* (Oxford: Oxford U.P., 1967), p. 3.
[4] Alexie, Sherman. *The Lone Ranger and Tonto Fistfight in Heaven.* (New York: Atlantic Monthly Press, 1993), p. 151.
[5] Zamora, *Writing the Apocalypse: Historical Vision in Contemporary U.S. and Latin American Fiction*, p. 10.
[6] Kermode, *The Sense of an Ending: Studies in the Theory of Fiction*, p. 7.
[7] Ibid., p. 11.
[8] Ibid., p. 97.
[9] Ibid., p. 95.
[10] Auden, W. H., *The English Auden.* (London: Faber and Faber, 1977). p. 299.
[11] Kermode, *The Sense of an Ending: Studies in the Theory of Fiction*, p.95.
[12] "eschatology, n." *The Oxford English Dictionary. 2nd Ed. 1989.* (OED Online: Oxford U.P.), 9 Feb. 2006 <http://dictionary.oed.com/cgi/entry/49086621>.
[13] Kermode, *The Sense of an Ending: Studies in the Theory of Fiction*, p.6.
[14] Zamora, *Writing the Apocalypse: Historical Vision in Contemporary U.S. and Latin American Fiction*, pp. 177, 180.
[15] Limerick, Patricia Nelson. *Legacy of Conquest: The Unbroken Past of the American West.* (New York: Norton, 1987), p. 27.
[16] Proulx, Annie. *Bad Dirt: Wyoming Stories 2.* (New York: Scribner, 2004), pp. 67-68.
[17] Rafferty, Terrence. "'Bad Dirt': A Town with Three Bars." The New York *Times Book Review*. (5 Dec. 2004): 46-47.
[18] Yeats, W.B. *The Major Works* (Oxford: Oxford U.P., 1997), p. 502.
[19] Bloom, Howard. *Yeats* (New York: Oxford U.P., 1970), pp. 344-348.
[20] Dix, Andrew, "Escape Stories: Narratives and Native Americans in Sherman Alexie's *The Lone Ranger and Tonto Fistfight in Heaven*." Yearbook of English Studies (2001, 31): 159-160.
[21] Alexie, *The Lone Ranger and Tonto Fistfight in Heaven*, p. 153
[22] Diamond, Jared. *Collapse: How Societies Choose to Fail or Survive.* (London: Penguin., 2005), pp. 32, 56.
[23] Ibid, pp. 30, 28.
[24] *Holy Bible: New Revised Standard Version.* (Quickverse for Windows. Parsons Technology, Inc., 1992 – 1994), Mark 13:32.
[25] McCarthy, Cormac. *Blood Meridian: Or, The Evening Redness in the West.* (1st Vintage International ed. New York: Vintage Books, 1992), p. 146.

I: From the New World to New Western History and Literature

[1] Slotkin, Richard. *Regeneration Through Violence: The Mythology of the American Frontier, 1600-1800.* (Middletown: Wesleyan U.P., 1973), p. 16.

[2] Zamora, *Writing the Apocalypse: Historical Vision in Contemporary U.S. and Latin American Fiction,* pp. 7, 8.

[3] Ibid., pp. 8-9.

[4] Slotkin, *Regeneration Through Violence: The Mythology of the American Frontier, 1600-1800,* p. 129.

[5] Zamora, *Writing the Apocalypse: Historical Vision in Contemporary U.S. and Latin American Fiction,* p. 9.

[6] Slotkin, *Regeneration Through Violence: The Mythology of the American Frontier, 1600-1800,* p. 58.

[7] Ibid., p. 58.

[8] Ibid., p. 18.

[9] Etulain, Richard. *Writing Western History: Essays on Major Western Historians.* (Albuquerque: U. of New Mexico P., 1991), p. 4.

[10] Slotkin, *Regeneration Through Violence: The Mythology of the American Frontier, 1600-1800,* p. 101.

[11] Ibid., p. 562.

[12] Ibid., p. 18.

[13] McMurtry, *Sacagawea's Nickname: Essays on the American West,* p. 9.

[14] Adler, Mortimer J., ed. *The Annals of America. Conspectus I.* (Chicago: Encyclopaedia Britannica, Inc., 1968), p. 86.

[15] Slotkin, *Regeneration Through Violence: The Mythology of the American Frontier, 1600-1800,* p. 17.

[16] Ibid., p. 8.

[17] Turner, Frederick Jackson. *Frontier and Section: Selected Essays.* (Englewood Cliffs: Prentice Hall, 1961), pp. 37-38.

[18] Limerick, *Legacy of Conquest: The Unbroken Past of the American West,* pp. 17-30.

[19] Slotkin, *Regeneration Through Violence: The Mythology of the American Frontier, 1600-1800,* p. 558.

[20] Slotkin, Richard. *Gunfighter Nation: The Myth of the Frontier in Twentieth-Century America.* (New York: Atheneum; Toronto; New York: Maxwell Macmillan Canada; Maxwell Macmillan International, 1992), pp. 10-16.

[21] Etulain, *Writing Western History: Essays on Major Western Historians* , p. 5.

[22] McDowell, Bart. *The American Cowboy in Life and Legend.* (Washington D.C.: National Geographic Society, 1972), pp. 37. 40-41.

[23] Limerick, *Legacy of Conquest: The Unbroken Past of the American West,* pp. 17-30.

[24] Slotkin, *Gunfighter Nation: The Myth of the Frontier in Twentieth-Century America,* pp. 10-30.

[25] Brown, Bill, ed. *Reading the West: An Anthology of Dime Westerns.* (Boston: Bedford Books, 1997), pp. 5, 20-21, 27, 31.

[26] Ibid, p. 5.; Etulain, *Writing Western History: Essays on Major Western Historians,* pp. 5-6.

[27] Emmert, Scott. *Loaded Fictions: Social Critique in the Twentieth-Century Western.* (Moscow: U. of Idaho P., 1996), pp. 48-49.
[28] McMurtry, *Sacagawea's Nickname: Essays on the American West*, p. 6.
[29] Limerick, Patricia Nelson. *Trails: Toward a New Western History.* (Lawrence: U. P. of Kansas, 1991), pp. 85-86.
[30] Limerick, *Legacy of Conquest: The Unbroken Past of the American West*, pp. 17-30.
[31] Cook-Lynn, Elizabeth. *Why I Can't Read Wallace Stegner and Other Essays: A Tribal Voice.* (Madison: U of Wisconsin P., 1996), pp. 29-40.

II: Annie Proulx

[1] Proulx, *Bad Dirt: Wyoming Stories 2*, p. 68.
[2] Harrison, M. John, " A lot of bad geography: The ranchers and barkeeps of Annie Proulx's real Wyoming." *Times Literary Supplement* (3 Dec. 2004): 21.
[3] Rood, Karen Lane. *Understanding Annie Proulx.* (Columbia: U of South Carolina P., 2001), pp. 2, 9-10.
[4] Harrison, "A lot of bad geography", 21.
[5] Rafferty, "'Bad Dirt': A Town with Three Bars.", 46-47.
[6] Kermode, *The Sense of an Ending: Studies in the Theory of Fiction*, p.179.
[7] Rafferty, "'Bad Dirt': A Town with Three Bars.", 46-47.
[8] Ibid., 46-47.
[9] Proulx, *Bad Dirt: Wyoming Stories 2*, pp. 56-57.
[10] Rood, *Understanding Annie Proulx,* p. 11.
[11] Proulx, *Bad Dirt: Wyoming Stories 2*, pp. 17, 22-23.
[12] Ibid., pp. 23, 19.
[13] Ibid., pp. 30, 35, 43.
[14] Ibid., pp. 39, 37, 45.
[15] Ibid., p. 95.
[16] Abbey, Edward. *Desert Solitaire: A Season in the Wilderness.* (1st Touchstone ed. New York: Simon & Schuster, 1990), p. 48.
[17] Proulx, *Bad Dirt: Wyoming Stories 2*, p. 119.
[18] Ibid., pp. 110, 119-121, 123.
[19] Ibid., p. 116.
[20] Ibid., p. 124.
[21] Rafferty, "'Bad Dirt': A Town with Three Bars.", 46-47.
[22] Proulx, Annie. *Close Range: Wyoming Stories.* (New York: Scribner, 1999), pp. 107-108.
[23] Kermode, *The Sense of an Ending: Studies in the Theory of Fiction*, p. 27.
24 Sites, Kevin. "Rolling in Cash" Yahoo.com. (20 Nov. 2007). <http://potw.news.yahoo.com/s/potw/55334/rolling-in-cash>
[25] Rafferty, "'Bad Dirt': A Town with Three Bars.", 46-47.
[26] Proulx, *Bad Dirt: Wyoming Stories 2*, p. 65.
[27] Ibid., pp. 64, 68.
[28] Ibid., pp. 62-63.

²⁹ Ibid., p. 72.
³⁰ Rood, *Understanding Annie Proulx*, p. 11.
³¹ Proulx, *Bad Dirt: Wyoming Stories 2*, p. 67.
³² Ibid., p. 67.
³³ Ibid., p. 80–81.
³⁴ Ibid., p. 86.
³⁵ Ibid., p. 76.
³⁶ Baudrillard, Jean. *The Illusion of the End*. (Cambridge: Polity Press, 1994), p. 8.
37 Proulx, *Bad Dirt: Wyoming Stories 2*, pp. 86, 92.

III: Cormac McCarthy

¹ Gorra, Michael. "Journey into a land beyond law: Cormac McCarthy's busted deal." *Times Literary Supplement*. (28 Oct. 2005): 21.
² McCarthy, Cormac. *No Country For Old Men*. (New York: Knopf, 2005), pp. 3-4.
³ Kirn, Walter. "'No Country For Old Men': Texas Noir." The New York *Times Book Review*. (24 Jul. 2005)
⁴ McCarthy, *No Country For Old Men*, pp. 218, 159.
⁵ Ibid., pp. 298, 303-304
⁶ Ibid., p. 299.
⁷ Gorra, "Journey into a land beyond law", 21.
⁸ Brewton, Vince. "The Changing Landscape of Violence in Cormac McCarthy's early novels and The Border Trilogy." Southern Literary Journal 37 (2004): 134, 136.
⁹ Gorra, "Journey into a land beyond law", 21.
¹⁰ Gorra, "Journey into a land beyond law", 21.
¹¹ McCarthy, *No Country For Old Men*, p. 174.
¹² Ibid., p. 7.
¹³ Ibid., pp. 260, 259.
¹⁴ McCarthy, *Blood Meridian*, pp. 249-250.
¹⁵ McCarthy, *No Country For Old Men*, p. 260.
¹⁶ Gorra, "Journey into a land beyond law", 21.
¹⁷ McCarthy, *No Country For Old Men*, p. 177.
¹⁸ Ibid, p. 253; McCarthy, *Blood Meridian*, p. 198.
¹⁹ Kirn, "'No Country For Old Men': Texas Noir."
²⁰ McCarthy, *No Country For Old Men*, p. 256.
²¹ Ibid., p. 248.
²² Gorra, "Journey into a land beyond law", 21.
²³ McCarthy, *No Country For Old Men*, p. 52.
²⁴ Gorra, "Journey into a land beyond law", 21.
²⁵ Kirn, "'No Country For Old Men': Texas Noir."
²⁶ Johnson, Michael L. *New Westers: The West in Contemporary American Culture*. (Lawrence: U. P. of Kansas, 1996), p. 145.

²⁷ Brewton, Vince. "The Changing Landscape of Violence in Cormac McCarthy's early novels and The Border Trilogy," 123.
²⁸ McCarthy, *No Country For Old Men*, pp. 182, 112.
29 Ibid., p. 210.
³⁰ Ibid., pp. 295, 306, 309.
³¹ Ibid., p. 31.
³² McCarthy, Cormac. *The Road*. (London: Picador, 2006), p. 75.

IV: Sherman Alexie

¹ Alexie, *The Lone Ranger and Tonto Fistfight in Heaven*, p. 55.
² Millard, Kenneth. *Contemporary American Fiction*. (Oxford; New York: Oxford U.P., 2000.), p. 100.
³ Alexie, *The Lone Ranger and Tonto Fistfight in Heaven*, pp. 51-54.
⁴ Ibid., p. 40.
⁵ Proulx, *Bad Dirt: Wyoming Stories 2*, p. 40.
⁶ Alexie, *The Lone Ranger and Tonto Fistfight in Heaven*, p. 119.
⁷ Cook-Lynn, *Why I Can't Read Wallace Stegner and Other Essays: A Tribal Voice*, pp. 29-40.
⁸ Proulx, *Bad Dirt: Wyoming Stories 2*, p. 199.
⁹ McCarthy, *Blood Meridian*, p. 146.
¹⁰ Alexie, *The Lone Ranger and Tonto Fistfight in Heaven*, p. 119.
¹¹ Torrez, Juliette. "Juliette Torrez goes Long Distance with Sherman Alexie." Poetry.com. (21 Feb. 2005).
<http://poetry.about.com/library/weekly/aa083199.htm?once=true&terms=alexie>
¹² Alexie, *The Lone Ranger and Tonto Fistfight in Heaven*, pp. 8, 81.
¹³ Dix, "Escape Stories: Narratives and Native Americans in Sherman Alexie's *The Lone Ranger and Tonto Fistfight in Heaven*," 158.
¹⁴ Johnson, *New Westers*, p. 152.
¹⁵ Alexie, *The Lone Ranger and Tonto Fistfight in Heaven*, p. 164.
¹⁶ Kermode, *The Sense of an Ending: Studies in the Theory of Fiction*, p. 155.
¹⁷ Alexie, *The Lone Ranger and Tonto Fistfight in Heaven*, pp. 176, 182-186.
¹⁸ Ibid., p. 187.
¹⁹ Kermode, *The Sense of an Ending: Studies in the Theory of Fiction*, p. 8.
²⁰ Alexie, *The Lone Ranger and Tonto Fistfight in Heaven*, pp. 186-187, 189-190.
²¹ Ibid., p. 149.
²² Dix, "Escape Stories: Narratives and Native Americans in Sherman Alexie's *The Lone Ranger and Tonto Fistfight in Heaven*," 162.
²³ Alexie, *The Lone Ranger and Tonto Fistfight in Heaven*, pp. 79-80.
²⁴ Campbell, Neil. *Cultures of the American New West*. (Edinburgh: Edinburgh U.P., 2000), p. 110.
²⁵ Alexie, *The Lone Ranger and Tonto Fistfight in Heaven*, pp. 149-150.
²⁶ Millard, *Contemporary American Fiction*, p. 98.
²⁷ Alexie, *The Lone Ranger and Tonto Fistfight in Heaven*, p. 152.

[28] Ibid., pp. 151-153.
[29] Ibid., pp. 140-141.
[30] Dix, "Escape Stories: Narratives and Native Americans in Sherman Alexie's *The Lone Ranger and Tonto Fistfight in Heaven*," 162.
[31] DeNuccio, Jerome. "Slow Dancing with Skeletons: Sherman Alexie's *The Lone Ranger and Tonto Fistfight in Heaven*." Critique. (Fall 2002, Vol. 44, Issue I): 90.
[32] Dix, "Escape Stories: Narratives and Native Americans in Sherman Alexie's *The Lone Ranger and Tonto Fistfight in Heaven*," 166.
[33] Alexie, *The Lone Ranger and Tonto Fistfight in Heaven*, pp. 22, 122.
[34] DeNuccio, Jerome. "Slow Dancing with Skeletons: Sherman Alexie's *The Lone Ranger and Tonto Fistfight in Heaven*," 97.

Conclusion: Beyond Apocalypse—
Western Places and Myths in the 21st Century

[1] Zamora, *Writing the Apocalypse: Historical Vision in Contemporary U.S. and Latin American Fiction*, p. 176.
[2] McMurtry, *Sacagawea's Nickname: Essays on the American West*, p. 13.
[3] Ibid., pp. 4, 13.
[4] Emmert, *Loaded Fictions: Social Critique in the Twentieth-Century Western*, p. 149.
[5] Woodward, Richard B. "Cormac McCarthy's Venomous Fiction." The New York Times Book Review. 19 Apr. 1992.
[6] Zamora, *Writing the Apocalypse: Historical Vision in Contemporary U.S. and Latin American Fiction*, p. 177.
[7] Woodward, "Cormac McCarthy's Venomous Fiction."
[8] Kakutani, Michiko. "On the Loose in Badlands: Killer with a Cattle Gun." The New York *Times Book Review*. 18 Jul. 2005.
[9] Foucault, Michel. "Nietzsche, Genealogy, History." *Language, Counter-Memory, Practice: Selected Interviews and Essays.* Ed. D. F. Bouchard. (Ithaca: Cornell U.P., 1977), p. 151.
[10] Gorra, "Journey into a land beyond law", 21.
[11] Millard, *Contemporary American Fiction*, p. 108.
[12] Brewton, Vince. "The Changing Landscape of Violence in Cormac McCarthy's early novels and The Border Trilogy," 132.
[13] McCarthy, *No Country For Old Men*, p. 295.
[14] Slotkin, *Gunfighter Nation: The Myth of the Frontier in Twentieth-Century America*, pp. 643, 562.
[15] Meo, Nick. "Kabul's Colonel Kurtz." 2004. *Sunday Herald*. (1 Jun. 2006). <http://www.sundayherald.com/43285>
[16] McCarthy, *No Country For Old Men*, p. 295.
[17] Campbell, *Cultures of the American New West*, p. 29.
[18] Brezosky, Lynn. "College Offers Degree in Master Ranching." Yahoo.com. (22 Sept. 2007).

< http://biz.yahoo.com/ap/070922/master_ranchers.html?.v=2>
[19] Rafferty, "'Bad Dirt': A Town with Three Bars.", 46-47.
[20] qtd. in Rood, *Understanding Annie Proulx*, p. 9.
[21] Proulx, *Bad Dirt: Wyoming Stories 2*, p. 103.
[22] Proulx, *Close Range: Wyoming Stories*, p. 275
[23] Proulx, *Bad Dirt: Wyoming Stories 2*, p. 104.
[24] Kermode, *The Sense of an Ending: Studies in the Theory of Fiction*, pp. 27, 88.
[25] Cooper, David E. *World Philosophies: An Historical Introduction, 2nd Edition*. (Malden: Blackwell, 2003), pp. 448-449.
[26] Baudrillard, Jean. *America*. (London: Verso, 1988), p. 31.
[27] qtd. in Zamora, *Writing the Apocalypse: Historical Vision in Contemporary U.S. and Latin American Fiction*, pp. 190-191.
[28] Johnson, Michael L. *Hunger for the Wild: America's Obsession with the Untamed West*. (Lawrence: U.P. of Kansas, 2007), p. 400.
[29] McCarthy, Cormac. *The Border Trilogy* (London: Picador, 2002), p. 603.
[30] Bhahba, Homi. *The Location of Culture*. (London, UK: Routledge, 1994), pp. 154-155.
[31] Campbell, Duncan. "The Voice of the New Tribes." *The Guardian*. Books.guardian.co.uk. (21 Feb. 2005).
<http://books.guardian.co.uk/review/story/0,12084,868123,00.html>
[32] Alexie, Sherman. *Ten Little Indians*. (New York: Grove Press, 2003), pp. 91, 93.
[33] Zamora, *Writing the Apocalypse: Historical Vision in Contemporary U.S. and Latin American Fiction*, p. 177.
[34] Kermode, *The Sense of an Ending: Studies in the Theory of Fiction*, p. 25.
[35] Zamora, *Writing the Apocalypse: Historical Vision in Contemporary U.S. and Latin American Fiction*, p. 191.
[36] Pabst, Georgia. "Alexie Sends Strong Signals." Journal Sentinel, Inc. Jsonline.com. (21 Feb. 2005).
<http://www.jsonline.com/enter/books/mar02/25632.asp>
[37] Campbell, *Cultures of the American New West*, p. 112.
[38] Kermode, *The Sense of an Ending: Studies in the Theory of Fiction*, p. 179.

Works Cited
Primary Materials

Abbey, Edward. *Desert Solitaire : A Season in the Wilderness.* 1st Touchstone ed. New York: Simon & Schuster, 1990.

Alexie, Sherman. *The Lone Ranger and Tonto Fistfight in Heaven.* New York: Atlantic Monthly Press, 1993.

—. *Ten Little Indians.* New York: Grove Press, 2003.

—. "Public Address." Hall of Presidents, Colgate University, Hamilton. 3 Nov. 2004.

Auden, W. H. *The English Auden.* London: Faber and Faber, 1977.

Eliot, T. S. *Collected Poems 1909-1962.* Orlando: Harcourt Brace & Company, 1963.

Holy Bible: New Revised Standard Version. Craig Rairdin. Quickverse for Windows. Parsons Technology, Inc. 1992-1994.

McCarthy, Cormac. *Blood Meridian, Or, the Evening Redness in the West.* 1st Vintage International, ed. New York: Vintage Books, 1992.

—. *No Country For Old Men.* New York: Knopf, 2005.

—. *The Border Trilogy.* London: Picador, 2002.

—. *The Road.* London: Picador, 2006.

Proulx, Annie. "A Week Out of the Wind—Part II." Annieproulx.com. 21 February 2005. <http://www.annieproulx.com/essay_may_2003.html>

---. *Bad Dirt : Wyoming Stories 2.* New York: Scribner, 2004.

---. *Close Range : Wyoming Stories.* New York: Scribner, 1999.

Yeats, W.B. *The Major Works.* Oxford: Oxford U.P., 1997.

Secondary Materials Cited & Consulted

Adler, Mortimer J., ed. *The Annals of America. Conspectus I*. Chicago: Encyclopaedia Britannica, Inc., 1968.

Baudrillard, Jean. *America*. London: Verso, 1988.

— *The Illusion of the End*. Cambridge: Polity Press, 1994.

Bhabha, Homi. *The Location of Culture*. London, UK: Routledge, 1994.

Bloom, Harold. *Yeats*. New York: Oxford U. P., 1970.

Bos, Truus. "Difficulty of enforcing law in lawless land." 2004. MSNBC.com. 1 Jun. 2006. < http://www.msnbc.msn.com/id/5771458/>

Brewton, Vince. "The Changing Landscape of Violence in Cormac McCarthy's early novels and the Border Triolgy." *Southern Literary Journal* 37 (2004): 121-143.

Brown, Bill, ed. *Reading the West : An Anthology of Dime Westerns*. Boston: Bedford Books, 1997.

Brezosky, Lynn. "College Offers Degree in Master Ranching." Yahoo.com. 22 Sept. 2007. < http://biz.yahoo.com/ap/070922/master_ranchers.html?.v=2>

Campbell, Duncan. "The Voice of the New Tribes." *The Guardian*. Books.guardian.co.uk. 21 February 2005. <http://books.guardian.co.uk/review/story/0,12084,868123,00.html>

Campbell, Neil. *The Cultures of the American New West*. Edinburgh: Edinburgh U. P., 2000.

Cook-Lynn, Elizabeth. *Why I can't Read Wallace Stegner and Other Essays : A Tribal Voice*. Madison: U. of Wisconsin P., 1996.

Cooper, David E. *World Philosophies: An Historical Introduction, 2nd Edition*. Malden: Blackwell, 2003.

DeNuccio, Jerome. "Slow Dancing with Skeletons: Sherman Alexie's *The Lone Ranger and Tonto Fistfight in Heaven*." Critique, Fall 2002, Vol. 44, Issue 1, p. 86-97.

Diamond, Jared. *Collapse: How Societies Choose to Fail or Survive*. London: Penguin, 2005.

Dix, Andrew. "Escape Stories: Narratives and Native Americans in Sherman Alexie's *The Lone Ranger and Tonto Fistfight in Heaven.*" Yearbook of English Studies 2001, 31, 155-67.

"eschatology, *n."* *The Oxford English Dictionary.* 2nd ed. 1989. OED Online. Oxford University Press. 9 Feb. 2006 <http://dictionary.oed.com/cgi/entry/49086621>.

Emmert, Scott. *Loaded Fictions : Social Critique in the Twentieth-Century Western.* Moscow, Idaho: U. of Idaho P., 1996.

Etulain, Richard. *Writing Western History: Essays on Major Western Historians.* Albuquerque: U. of New Mexico P., 1991.

Foucault, Michel. "Nietzsche, Genealogy, History." *Language, Counter-Memory, Practice: Selected Interviews and Essays.* Ed. D. F. Bouchard. Ithaca: Cornell U.P., 1977.

Gorra, Michael. "Journey into a land beyond law: Cormac McCarthy's busted deal." *Times Literary Supplement.* 28 Oct. 2005: 21.

Harrison, M. John. "A lot of bad geography: The ranchers and barkeeps of Annie Proulx's real Wyoming." *Times Literary Supplement.* 3 Dec. 2004: 21.

Johnson, Michael L. *Hunger for the Wild: America's Obsession with the Untamed West.* Lawrence: U. P. of Kansas, 2007.

—. *New Westers: The West in Contemporary American Culture.* Lawrence: U. P. of Kansas, 1996.

Kakutani, Michiko. "On the Loose in Badlands: Killer with a Cattle Gun." The New York *Times Book Review.* 18 Jul. 2005.

Kermode, Frank. *The Sense of an Ending: Studies in the Theory of Fiction.* Oxford: Oxford U.P., 1967.

Kirn, Walter. "'No Country For Old Men': Texas Noir." The New York *Times Book Review.* 24 Jul. 2005.

Limerick, Patricia Nelson. *The Legacy of Conquest : The Unbroken Past of the American West.* New York: Norton, 1987.

—. *Trails: Toward A New Western History.* Lawrence: U. P. of Kansas, 1991.

McDowell, Bart. *The American Cowboy in Life and Legend.* Washington D.C.: National Geographic Society, 1972.

McMurtry, Larry. *Sacagawea's Nickname: Essays on the American West.* New York: New York Review of Books, 2001.

Meo, Nick. "Kabul's Colonel Kurtz." 2004. *Sunday Herald.* 1 Jun. 2006. <http://www.sundayherald.com/43285>

Millard, Kenneth. *Contemporary American Fiction.* Oxford; New York: Oxford U. P., 2000.

Pabst, Georgia. "Alexie Sends Strong Signals." Journal Sentinel, Inc. Jsonline.com. 21 February 2005. <http://www.jsonline.com/enter/books/mar02/25632.asp>

Rafferty, Terrence. "'Bad Dirt': A Town with Three Bars." The New York Times Book Review. 5 Dec. 2004: 46-47.

Rood, Karen Lane. *Understanding Annie Proulx.* Columbia: U. of South Carolina P., 2001.

Sites, Kevin. "Rolling in Cash." Yahoo.com. 20 Nov. 2007. <http://potw.news.yahoo.com/s/potw/55334/rolling-in-cash>

Slotkin, Richard. *Gunfighter Nation : The Myth of the Frontier in Twentieth-Century America.* New York : Atheneum ; Toronto; New York: Maxwell Macmillan Canada; Maxwell Macmillan International, 1992.

—. *Regeneration Through Violence: The Mythology of the American Frontier, 1600-1800.* Middletown: Wesleyan U.P., 1973.

"The Wild Frontier." 2006. Guardian.co.uk. 1 Jun. 2006. <http://www.guardian.co.uk/g2/story/0,,1698471,00.html>

"The Wild West: Barwana and Ramadi." *The Economist.* 6 Apr. 2006.

Tompkins, Jane. *West of Everything: The Inner Life of Westerns.* Oxford: Oxford U.P., 1992.

Torrez, Juliette. "Juliette Torrez goes Long Distance with Sherman Alexie." Poetry.com. 21 February 2005. <http://poetry.about.com/library/weekly/aa083199.htm?once=true&terms=alexie>

Turner, Frederick Jackson. *Frontier and Section; Selected Essays.* Englewood Cliffs: Prentice Hall, 1961.

Woodward, Richard B. "Cormac McCarthy's Venomous Fiction." The New York *Times Book Review.* 19 Apr. 1992

Zamora, Lois Parkinson. *Writing the Apocalypse: Historical Vision in Contemporary U.S. and Latin American Fiction.* Cambridge: Cambridge U.P., 1989.

About the Author

JEREMY T. WATTLES was born and raised in Central New York. A graduate of Colgate University and the University of Edinburgh, he is an avid long distance runner, fiction writer, and poet. He lives in Geneva, New York.

www.ingramcontent.com/pod-product-compliance
Lightning Source LLC
LaVergne TN
LVHW011429080426
835512LV00005B/352